San Juan Classics

San Juan Classics

COOKBOOK

Dawn Ashbach

Janice Veal

Island Publishers

ANACORTES, WASHINGTON

Printed in the United States of America
7th printing

Cover photograph, *San Juan Islands* by Matt Brown
Title lettering by Nancy Jang.

Library of Congress Cataloging-in-Publication Data

Ashbach, Dawn, 1948-
   San Juan classics cookbook.

   Includes index.
   1. Cookery – Washington (State) – San Juan Islands.
I. Veal, Janice, 1947-   . II. Title.
TX715.A775 1987   641.5   87-3420
ISBN 0-9615580-2-4

Table of Contents

This book is dedicated to our families whose continued support and healthy appetites have made this book possible. Many thanks to Bud, Matt and Brian Ashbach and Glen, Adam and Eric Veal.

Preface

This cookbook features a special cuisine, reflective of the natural abundance, rich history and relaxed lifestyle which has evolved in the San Juan Islands. Like the native Indians and early pioneers, islanders today use the bounty of the land and surrounding seas. The aroma and flavor of oysters on the grill, salmon smoking over alder wood and wild blackberry pie are all natural fare for San Juan residents. To these natural ingredients we have added the classic cuisine and ethnic variations that reflect the heritage of the pioneers and later inhabitants of these islands. Combining these elements, we offer you some mouthwatering tastes from the region. Our book includes recipes from fine island cooks and selected island restaurants, as well as our own collections derived from 17 years of enjoying the abundance of the San Juan Islands.

Dawn Ashbach and Janice Veal
Guemes Island, WA

Restaurants

We wish to thank the following restaurants for generously sharing some of their favorite recipes:

ORCAS ISLAND
Bilbo's Festivo
Christina's
La Famiglia Ristorante
Rosario Resort

SAN JUAN ISLAND
Cafe Bissett
Downriggers Restaurant
Roche Harbor Restaurant
Winston's Restaurant

LOPEZ ISLAND
Jeanna's Seafood Gallery
New Bay Cafe

FIDALGO ISLAND
La Petite Restaurant
Slocum's

LA CONNER
Barkley's of La Conner

Acknowledgements

We would like to express our sincere thanks to those people who have made this book possible. To our publishers, Delphine Haley and Thelma Palmer, for their advice and assistance. To Clifford Burke, who provided his expertise and encouragement. To Betty Crookes and Kris Molesworth, whose editing was most helpful. To Peter Capen, Matt Brown and Joella Solus, for their outstanding photographs. To Cleo Bratt and Barbara Hoenselaar, whose typing enabled us to meet our deadlines.

To our families and old and new friends for sharing their favorite recipes: Mick Allen, Elaine Anderson, Bud Ashbach, Claudia Ashbach, Lee Ashbach, Shirley Baier, Teresa Benjamin, Dorothy Bird, Peggy Bisordi, Cleo Bratt, Yuriko Bullock, Laura Burton, Sylvia Carrieri of Olympic Lights on San Juan Island, Cherie Christensen, Ellen Christensen, Chris Damarjian, Joanne Funk, Rob Girdis, Cindy Gugich, Christine Hale, Peter Heffelfinger, Ken Jacot, Anastasia Karageorges, Scott McCullough, Anne McCracken, Jane Nelson, Darrell Palmer, Noel Paus, Jane Read, Betty Rice of Wharfside Bed and Breakfast in Friday Harbor, Samish Indian Office, Sarah Spaeth, Mitzi Stack of Tucker House on San Juan Island, Melita Townsend, Bill and Doe Webb, Kim Weil, Rita Yantorni and Yadira Young.

The San Juan Islands

Stuart I.

Waldron I.

Speiden I.

ORCAS ISLAND

Lummi I.

SHAW ISLAND

Sinclair I.

SAN JUAN
ISLAND

Blakely I.

Cypress I.

Guemes I.

Decatur I.

LOPEZ
ISLAND

FIDALGO
ISLAND

Life in the San Juans

by Delphine Haley

Islands are magical places. And when they form an archipelago, the magic intensifies. In few other places is this more apparent than in the Pacific Northwest, where a cluster of geologic jewels – the San Juan Islands – lie scattered in an emerald inland sea. Here in this exquisite setting, the geology, the climate and the natural and human history have combined to form a distinct San Juan Islands culture.

The San Juan Islands that we see today are actually leftover mountaintops from an ancient range that once dominated this region. During the Ice Age, some 12,000 or more years ago, glaciers covered and carved through the region, leaving behind a maze of waterways punctuated by some 172 (depending upon the tide and the source consulted) granite and sandstone islands. Today they are crowned with firs, tinted with red barked madrona and the blossoms of rhododendron, laced with wildflowers and ferns and sculpted with varying shorelines. The waters that filled in after these glacial scourings – a mixture of saltwater from the Pacific and runoff from myriad rivers on the mainland – are now among the most fertile in the United States. Phytoplankton, the basic food source in the sea, blooms here in profusion, lending the waters an emerald hue. It is the basis for a rich food chain that extends from the tiniest protozoan all the way up to the largest whales. As a result, San Juan shores abound in shellfish – oysters, clams, crab and mussels – and the deeper waters are a home for octopus, herring, and various species of salmon and white fish.

Such abundance has blessed those who have occupied these magical islands. The early Indians, the Lummi and the Samish, lived a relatively easy life, governed by the seasons, the tides and the salmon runs. Clothed in woven or shredded cedar bark, they dug clams, roots and bulbs, gathered oysters, mussels and berries and fished from their dugout cedar canoes. The struggle for survival was minimal, except for the occasional raids of the

11

Haida or Tlingit to the north, leaving time for woodworking, weaving, basket making, canoe building and fashioning intricately designed reef nets. Such a bountiful lifestyle was reflected in the belief that human life had actually begun on San Juan Island and that these islands were sacred.

But the Indians' way of life was to be threatened. Eventually, "strange bearded men began to arrive in their huge canoes with white wings." In the early 1790's, Spanish explorers—Quimper, Pantoja, Galiano and Valdes—sailed among the San Juans and set their country's names upon the passages, headlands and islands. In 1792, the British under Captain George Vancouver began to chart the maze of channels and bays and give them names. Conflicting land claims between the Spanish and English almost led to a war, but finally a treaty in which the Spanish gave up all claim to the Pacific Northwest was signed in 1793. By the mid 1800's, white settlers were homesteading throughout the San Juans, and commerce, including a Hudson's Bay Company, was established. By this time too, the Americans had laid full claim to the area, and Captain John Wilkes' 1841 expedition added names to the landmarks not already claimed by the Spanish and English. Eventually ownership of the islands became an issue between the British and the Americans which resulted in a period of joint occupancy. It developed into a territorial rivalry which escalated into the infamous Pig War of 1859, where the only casualty was a pig. As a result of rising tensions between British and American settlers, military forces arrived on San Juan Island. American soldiers formed an armed camp at the southern tip of the island and the English set up camp at Garrison Bay on the northeast side of the island. Eventually the borders between Canada and the United States were peacefully settled, and in 1872 the British withdrew beyond Haro Strait. In the following year, many of the islands in the San Juans were organized into San Juan County, with the town of Friday Harbor on San Juan Island as its county seat.

The islands have supported a hardy breed of independent settlers ever since—people who have chosen a life that is not only isolated but insulated from the stresses of the mainland. Above all, San Juan islanders are independent. Beyond that, one learns not to generalize. In the early 1900's some of the early settlers were smugglers. The hidden coves and rugged coastlines made it possible for even the most respected citizen to smuggle foodstuffs, wool, liquor, opium and even people (in the form of Oriental laborers) back

12

and forth across the border. For the most part, however, islanders survived by fishing, logging and farming. Eventually, when transport costs made local products too expensive and mainland farms became more efficient, farming dwindled out as a common means of support. Commercial fishing, too, has suffered due to declining numbers of salmon and the impact of the Boldt Decision, which established quotas between commercial, sports and Indian fishermen.

Today some islanders support themselves with small businesses, some of which have been operating for several generations. Because of the fragmented population and the seasonal nature of the local economy, it is often a struggle for these ventures to survive. Construction is the dominant outdoor employment. The islands abound with small "cottage industries." Many writers and artists have found their creative energies influenced by the tranquility of the setting. The inconvenience of island living is compensated for, in part, by the sight of an eagle wheeling above, the sound of orcas as they surface off shore and the peaceful progression of the days.

Each island, no matter what its size, has distinctive qualities derived from its topography, coastline, vegetation, human history – even its prevailing winds and surrounding waters. These and other more subtle traits combine to give each island a special character or personality. Some are wild and desolate, temporary homes only for birds and seals; others are more ordered, their perimeters defined with paths and their hearts crisscrossed with roads and other signs of human habitation. Some islands emanate power from their cliffs and in the shadows of their rugged hills; others radiate tranquility from sunny meadows and along quiet bays.

Orcas Island, with its 57 square miles formed in the shape of a horseshoe, is the largest of the San Juans, and its terrain – mountains, lakes and endless shoreline – is probably the most varied. It has a full complement of shops and services in its five townships and many homes ranging from small cottages to palatial estates. Because of the many facilities available to visitors, Orcas has also been called the restaurant and resort island. Rosario Resort, a Victorian mansion built in the early 1900's and now expanded into a hotel-condo complex, is an elegant blend of the antique and modern. Nearby is Moran State Park which includes 5000 acres of woods, fresh-water lakes and saltwater shorelines, nearly 30 miles of trails and four waterfalls. The highlight of the park is Mount Constitution, the tallest peak in the San

Juans, which provides a sweeping vista of the San Juan Islands, the Canadian Gulf Islands, Vancouver Island, Mount Baker and even Mount Rainier, more than 140 miles away.

San Juan Island, six miles wide and ten miles long, is the second largest of the San Juans. With two centers of activity—one at the county seat of Friday Harbor on the east and the other at the resort and marina at Roche Harbor on the west. It is contrasted by rolling farmland, windswept fields and towering bluffs. These factors seem to lend the island a character that is both rural and commercial, old and new, natural and civilized. Wild natural areas, historic reminders and modern amenities are within a few miles or sometimes a few feet of each other. At the northern and southern ends of the island are the former English and American campsites from the Pig War of 1859. At the old company town of Roche Harbor, a pristine white church and the magnificent old Hotel de Haro (built in 1886) are flanked by an air strip, an Olympic-sized pool and a marina filled with modern pleasure boats. The city of Friday Harbor is a bustling Port of Entry, full of small shops, restaurants and a delightful Whale Museum. Lime Kiln Lighthouse on the west shore is a perfect land base for viewing wild orca whales and the windswept southern shores provide ideal birdwatching for eagles, hawks and seabirds.

Lopez Island has no identity problem. Primarily a friendly and tranquil island, with the greatest amount of tillable soil, its 47 square miles are characterized by orchards and farms. No large town has developed, but the island's three communities and its perimeters are connected by winding country roads that are favored by visiting cyclists. At its center is Hummel Lake, known for rainbow trout, and off its southern shore, seiners and trawlers raft up when not at work in the Strait. As the most southerly of the San Juan group, Lopez has a moderate climate which seems to fit with the mellow lifestyle of its inhabitants.

Shaw Island is at the center of the San Juan cluster, at 4,900 acres the smallest island served by the state ferry system. It too is a quiet rural community with no business center, except for a store run by the Franciscan nuns at the ferry landing. Shaw is almost entirely privately owned; the only public campground accommodates just a few visitors. Its 11 miles of roads wind along small fields bordered by hedgerows, alternating with heavy timber, residences and farmsteads.

These four largest islands are united by ferries that belong to the largest marine highway system in the world. But they are only a small representa-

14

tion of the myriad island jewels set in these green waters. Some, accessible only by plane, boat or two small county ferries, are inhabited by people, others are home only to wild animals and birds, and claimed by various agencies such as parks, preserves and some 64 designated wildlife refuges. *Waldron Island* is known for its independent character. With neither phone nor electricity, its 100 or so residents prefer to maintain their island relatively unaltered, thereby preserving a self-reliant way of life. *Cypress Island,* the last undeveloped island of the large San Juans, is a dramatic and mountainous presence among the group. Its steep rocky peaks, dense forests and high spring-fed lakes are a reminder of the untamed and original beauty of the San Juans. Next to it is *Guemes Island,* an often overlooked residential island whose spirit is as gentle and nurturing as that of Cypress is wild. To the north, rises the mountainous spine of *Lummi Island,* original home of the Lummi Indians. Its precipitous slopes turn gentle only on its northern side, where a few farms and residences are found. Other islands – *Decatur, Sinclair, Blakely* and *Center* – are owned by private groups, each with airstrips for quick access and escape from the mainland. *Fidalgo Island* is connected to the mainland by the Swinomish bridges and is often forgotten as an island. The town of Anacortes on Fidalgo is known as the "gateway to the San Juans," providing the terminus for the Washington State Ferry System and a journey through magical lands and waterways of unparalleled beauty.

Notes on Ingredients

Ingredients

CILANTRO – A uniquely flavored parsley. It is available fresh in the produce section or dried in the spice section of most supermarkets.

CREAM – Use whipping cream in recipes that list heavy cream, light cream refers to half-and-half. If the recipe includes wine or lemon, be sure to use whipping cream, as half-and-half will curdle. In many cases yogurt can be used as a low-calorie substitute for cream and mayonnaise.

HERBS – Most of our recipes call for dried herbs; if using fresh, use 3 times the given amount.

LEMON JUICE – May often be used as a healthful substitute for salt.

OIL – Olive oil or safflower oil can be substituted for butter, margarine or vegetable oil in most recipes as a healthful alternative.

PESTO SAUCE – If a recipe calls for a cube of Pesto Sauce, you may substitute 2 teaspoons dried basil, 1 tablespoon fresh minced parsley and 2 tablespoons olive oil.

WINE – Stocks, vegetable and fruit juices or water can be used as a substitute for recipes listing wine.

Cooking Terms

AL DENTE – Pasta cooked until tender but firm.

DEGLAZE – Add wine, stock or cream to a heated pan and loosen the residue with a spatula to create a sauce.

REDUCE – Cook a sauce or liquid until the volume is reduced and the flavor becomes concentrated.

SAUTÉ AND STIR-FRY – Place food in a hot pan with a small amount of oil and cook quickly.

Recipe Interpretations

CAPITALIZATIONS – Recipes that are included in the cookbook are capitalized in the list of ingredients.

INGREDIENTS – Recipes can always be altered according to the cook's preferences and availability of ingredients.

Appetizers

MATT BROWN

Ferry at Ship Harbor

Gravlax

Darrell Palmer, a former purser on the Washington State Ferry System, has refined this recipe over the past 20 years. It is his most requested recipe and we were delighted when he agreed to share it with us.

    2 salmon fillets, about 3 pounds
    ⅓ cup rock salt (if you double the recipe do not double salt)
    4 tablespoons sugar
    3 tablespoons dried dill weed, or 2 cups fresh dill sprigs
    1½ tablespoons white peppercorns, coarsely crushed
    ⅓ cup vegetable oil
    MUSTARD SAUCE (recipe follows)

1. Wash salmon fillets and pat dry with paper towel. Lay thickest fillet, skin side down, in a glass or ceramic baking dish just large enough to hold salmon.

2. Sprinkle salmon with salt, sugar, dill and pepper. Press seasonings into flesh. Carefully lay other fillet, skin side up, on top. Cover fillets with plastic wrap.

3. Place a small sheet of plywood on top of salmon and weigh it down with a couple of bricks or a 2 pound rock and refrigerate. (The pressure ensures a fine texture to the salmon.)

4. After 12 hours, carefully turn salmon while fillets are still together, so that the top fillet is on the bottom. Continue to turn salmon every 12 hours.

5. After 24 hours, pour oil over salmon; thereafter baste every time you turn it.

6. Check salmon after 48 hours to see if it is to your liking. This amount of salmon will probably take 3 days.

7. When salmon is "done," run it under cold water to rinse. Pat dry with paper towels.

8. Lay salmon on a cutting board and cut each fillet in half lengthwise. Using a sharp knife, cut salmon from tail to head into thin diagonal slices.

9. Arrange slices on a plate and serve with Mustard Sauce or with bagels and cream cheese. Your guests will rave.   12 servings

MUSTARD SAUCE
⅓ cup Dijon mustard
⅓ cup sugar
¾ teaspoon dried dill weed
¼ cup cider vinegar
¼ cup sour cream

In a small bowl, combine all ingredients. Cover and chill until ready to use. Sauce will keep for 4 days. 1 cup

Salmon Caviar

Next time you have a freshly caught female salmon, save the egg sac to make this sophisticated appetizer, given to us by Peter Heffelfinger. If you choose to make a different amount, maintain a 4 to 1 ratio of salt and water for the brine.

2 cups salmon roe (eggs)
1 cup canning salt (non-iodized)
4 cups cold water

1. Strip the membrane from the roe sac as gently as possible. Do not rinse eggs, as they will become soft.

2. In a large bowl, combine salt and water; add salmon eggs and swirl gently to allow the brine to reach all the eggs. Let stand for 20 to 30 minutes, no longer, as eggs may become too salty. Remove any remaining membrane, which will appear white in color.

3. Drain into a colander and immerse colander and eggs into a pan of ice-cold water. Drain again and allow to rest in the colander for 1 hour while in the refrigerator. Transfer to glass jars; use plastic wrap to form a protective seal with no air space. Cover with a tight-fitting lid and store in the refrigerator.

4. Serve caviar in bowl embedded in ice. Heap it on fresh toast cut into triangles and top with a squeeze of lemon. Caviar will keep for 2 months.

1 pint

Thank you
for your
support and attendance

W.A. Botting Company

MDC Critique

May 1-3, 1996

Salmon Pâté Medalions à la Rosario

Rosario mansion was built in the early 1900's by shipbuilder Robert Moran. This beautiful resort overlooks Cascade Bay which is filled with pleasure boats during the summer season. This delicate pâté is served in the Orcas Room for the Friday evening seafood buffet.

3 pounds raw salmon fillet, boned
6 egg whites
1/4 cup dry white wine
1/2 teaspoon Worcestershire sauce
2 teaspoons dried dill weed
Cayenne pepper, to taste
White pepper, to taste
1 cup heavy cream
1/2 cup rice flour

1. Finely chop salmon; place in a food processor and puree. Add egg whites, wine, Worcestershire sauce and seasonings; mix thoroughly, Remove salmon mixture from food processor and press through a fine sieve into a large bowl. Fold in cream and rice flour. Divide mixture into 3 portions.

2. Preheat oven to 325°. Spray 3 6x18-inch sheets of aluminum foil with non-stick coating. Using the aluminum foil, roll-up each portion into a tight roll, approximately 10-inches long. Twist ends of foil tightly.

3. Place rolls in a baking pan with 1-inch sides. Fill pan with 1/2-inch of hot water and bake for 25-30 minutes or until rolls are firm. Remove from water and allow to set up for 10 minutes. Cut into 1/4-1/2-inch slices with a serrated knife. Serve warm or refrigerate and use as a cold appetizer on toasted bread or crackers.   3 10-inch rolls

Salmon Stuffed Tomatoes

These enticing morsels add color to an appetizer tray.

2 pints cherry tomatoes
1 cup cooked salmon, bones and skin removed
2 tablespoons sour cream
2 tablespoons mayonnaise
1 tablespoon finely minced green onions
1 tablespoon minced fresh parsley
1 teaspoon dried dill weed
1 tablespoon chili sauce
2 teaspoons fresh lemon juice
1 teaspoon horseradish
1/4 teaspoon salt
Parsley sprigs

1. Cut tops off tomatoes and scoop out pulp and seeds. Turn upside down to drain.
2. In a medium bowl, combine all remaining ingredients and mix well.
3. Fill tomatoes with salmon mixture; cover and chill at least 1 hour. Garnish serving platter with parsley.   2 dozen

Salmon Pâté

This is a delicious way to use leftover cooked salmon. If using smoked salmon, omit liquid smoke.

8 ounces cream cheese
1 tablespoon lemon juice
2 teaspoons minced onion
1/4 teaspoon liquid smoke
1 teaspoon horseradish
1 cup cooked salmon, cooled
2 tablespoons chopped fresh parsley
Parsley sprigs

In a mixing bowl, blend all ingredients. Transfer to a serving bowl; cover and chill until needed. Garnish with parsley sprigs. Serve with crackers or party rye.   2 cups

Woodfired Oysters with Champagne Sauce

Cafe Bissett on San Juan Island offers these exquisite oysters as an appetizer or a light entree. This sophisticated restaurant provides innovative meals to the discriminating customer.

    1 cup champagne
    2 shallots, minced
    1 cup butter (2 cubes), chilled and cut into 8 pieces
    1 clove garlic, minced
    Salt and pepper, to taste
    2 large leeks, thinly julienned
    2 tablespoons clarified butter
    1 clove garlic, minced
    1 tablespoon minced parsley
    12 oysters, in the shell
    2 tablespoons black caviar

1. In a saucepan, simmer champagne and shallots over medium heat until liquid is reduced to 2 tablespoons. Over low heat, whisk in butter, one piece at a time, until melted. Stir in garlic; add salt and pepper and set aside.

2. In a small skillet, sauté leeks for 2 minutes in clarified butter. Add a pinch of garlic and parsley; set aside.

3. Wash oysters and place on a grill, cupped-side down, over an open wood fire that has reduced to a bed of coals. Cooking time depends upon temperature of the coals, but it should not take more than 3 to 4 minutes. When done, the oysters will start to bubble around the opening edges.

4. Open shells with an oyster knife and transfer oysters, including bottom shell, to serving plates. Ladle champagne sauce over oysters. Place leeks on top of each oyster and sprinkle each with ¼ teaspoon of caviar. Serve immediately and enjoy!   4 servings

Crumbed Oysters

These oysters are simply delicious.

¼ cup butter
1 clove garlic, minced
¾ cup seasoned dry bread crumbs
2 tablespoons chopped fresh parsley

2 dozen small raw oysters
3 tablespoons grated Parmesan cheese
4 drops Tabasco sauce
Lemon wedges

1. In a small saucepan, melt 2 tablespoons of butter; add garlic and crumbs. Sauté until golden. Stir in parsley.

2. Preheat oven to 450°. Spread two-thirds of bread mixture into shallow baking dish. Arrange oysters in one layer. Mix remaining crumbs with Parmesan and Tabasco and sprinkle on top of oysters. Dot oysters with remaining butter.

3. Bake for 15 minutes. Garnish with lemon. Serve hot with toothpicks.   2 dozen oysters

Big Lee's Hot Crab Dip

After a long day biking in the islands, Lee enjoys serving this to his friends.

1 (8-ounce) package cream cheese, at room temperature
¼ cup milk
1 tablespoon mayonnaise
2 tablespoons chili sauce
3 drops Tabasco sauce
2 tablespoons minced onions
½ teaspoon dry mustard
¼ teaspoon salt
3 tablespoons sliced green olives
1 cup cooked crab

1. Preheat oven to 375°. In a medium mixing bowl, combine all ingredients, except olives and crab; mix well.

2. Gently fold in olives and crab; spread into an 8-inch baking dish. Bake for 15 minutes. Serve hot with crackers or corn chips.   2½ cups

Crab Stuffed Mushrooms

Stuffed mushrooms are a perfect finger food. This is a prize-winning recipe.

2 dozen large fresh mushrooms (about 1 pound)
$\frac{1}{4}$ cup margarine or butter
1 clove garlic, minced
4 green onions, minced
1 cup soft bread crumbs
1 tablespoon chopped fresh parsley
1 cup cooked crab meat
1 tablespoon mayonnaise
1 tablespoon fresh lemon juice
1 teaspoon salt
$\frac{1}{8}$ teaspoon freshly ground pepper
2 tablespoons grated Parmesan cheese

1. Wash mushrooms; remove caps and set aside. Finely chop stems and set aside.

2. In a medium saucepan, melt margarine over medium heat. Sauté garlic, onion and mushroom stems until softened, about 5 minutes. Remove from heat and set aside.

3. Preheat oven to 425°. Stir in bread crumbs, parsley and crab meat. Gently fold in mayonnaise, lemon juice, salt and pepper.

4. Stuff mushroom caps with crab mixture and place on greased baking pan. Garnish with Parmesan. Bake for 10 minutes or until golden; serve hot.

2 dozen

Cheese Boerags

When Chris Damarjian of Guemes Island brings cheese boerags to island parties, they are everyone's favorite appetizers. Carefully follow package directions for phyllo dough. Dough should thaw in refrigerator for 2 days before using.

1 pound frozen phyllo dough, thawed according to package directions
8 ounces cottage cheese, cream-style
8 ounces Meunster cheese, grated
4 ounces Romano cheese, grated
4 ounces blue cheese, crumbled
2 eggs, slightly beaten
½ cup finely chopped parsley
½ teaspoon dried dill weed (optional)
8 ounces sweet butter, melted

1. In a medium bowl, combine cheeses, eggs, parsley and dill weed.

2. Remove phyllo from package; place sheets on flat surface and cover with plastic wrap to keep from drying out.

3. Remove 1 sheet of phyllo; place on flat surface and brush with melted butter. Cover first sheet with second sheet and brush with butter again.

4. Cut double sheets into 3 lengthwise strips for medium pastries or 4 lengthwise strips for small pastries.

5. Preheat oven to 375°. Place 1½ teaspoons of filling at one end of strip for medium pastries or 1 teaspoon filling for small. Fold a corner of the sheet over the filling to form a triangle. Continue folding end-over-end to the end of the strip. Brush top of each triangle with melted butter.

6. Arrange the boerags on an ungreased baking sheet. Bake for 20-25 minutes until golden. Serve warm.   50 medium

Tips for freezing boerags:

Boerags can be made in advance and frozen before baking. Brush the surface with melted butter and place on ungreased baking sheet. Cover tightly with plastic wrap and freeze. Transfer frozen boerags to plastic bags until needed. Do not defrost; they become soggy. Place frozen boerags on ungreased baking sheet and bake at 375° for 30 minutes.

Marinated Chicken Wings

It is difficult to resist this tantalizing appetizer.

    1/4 cup dry white wine
    1/4 cup soy sauce
    1/4 cup catsup
    1/4 cup salad oil
    1 tablespoon brown sugar
    1 teaspoon Worcestershire sauce
    2 cloves garlic, minced
    16 whole chicken wings, tips removed and wings cut at joint

1. In a large bowl, combine all ingredients for marinade. Marinate chicken for approximately 4 hours.

2. Preheat oven to 325°. Line large shallow baking dish with foil and arrange chicken in dish. Bake for 1 1/2 hours. Baste and turn every 30 minutes. Remove from oven and transfer to a serving platter. Serve hot or cold.

32 pieces

Winston's Stuffed Mushrooms

Winston's Restaurant, located in Friday Harbor on San Juan Island, serves these delectable appetizers to delighted patrons.

1/2 pound ricotta cheese
1/2 pound cream cheese
1 egg yolk
1/2 tablespoon minced garlic
1/2 tablespoon dried basil
1/2 tablespoon minced fresh parsley
1 teaspoon dried oregano
1/2 cup minced green onions
1/2 teaspoon freshly ground pepper
2 dozen mushrooms, cleaned and stems removed
1/4 cup butter
1-2 tablespoons minced garlic
1/4 cup dry sherry

1. In a large bowl, combine ricotta, cream cheese and egg yolk until well blended. Mix in next 6 ingredients until smooth; set aside.

2. Stuff mushrooms with cheese mixture and place in a baking pan. (Mushrooms may be refrigerated at this time.)

3. Preheat oven to 425°. In a small skillet, over medium heat, melt butter and sauté garlic for 1 minute, remove from heat and add sherry; stir to blend. Pour sauce over mushrooms just before baking.

4. Bake mushrooms for 15 minutes or until top is bubbly and well browned. Serve immediately.   2 dozen

Country Meatballs

Cherie Christensen serves these tasty meatballs as an appetizer to Shaw Island friends.

1 pound ground venison, lamb or beef
1/2 cup dry bread crumbs
1/3 cup minced onion
1 egg, slightly beaten
1 tablespoon minced fresh parsley
1 teaspoon Worcestershire sauce
1/2 teaspoon salt
1/4 teaspoon pepper
2 tablespoons vegetable oil
1 cup blackberry jelly or red currant jelly
1 cup bottled chili sauce

1. In a large bowl, mix together first 8 ingredients. Shape mixture into 1-inch balls. In a large skillet, heat oil and brown meatballs, turning gently.

2. With a slotted spoon, remove meatballs and drain on paper towels. Drain oil from pan and discard. Add jelly and chili sauce to pan; mix and heat through. Add meatballs and stir until thoroughly coated. Simmer for 1/2 hour, uncovered. Serve warm with toothpicks.   4 dozen

Eggplant Pâté

If you like eggplant, you'll love this pâté. Serve with pita bread, fresh vegetables or crackers.

2 medium eggplants, stems removed
1/2 cup tahini (sesame seed paste)*
3 tablespoons fresh lemon juice
2-3 cloves garlic, minced
1/2 cup chopped fresh parsley
2 tablespoons minced green onions
1 cup yogurt
1/2 teaspoon cumin
Dash cayenne pepper
1 teaspoon salt
1/2 teaspoon coarsely ground pepper
1 tablespoon olive oil

1. Preheat oven to 375°. Place eggplants on baking sheet; pierce skins with fork to avoid bursting. Bake for 1 hour or until very soft.

2. When cool, peel and place pulp in large bowl or food processor. Add remaining ingredients, except oil. Process or mash together until well blended. Add additional seasoning to taste.

3. Pour pâté into serving bowl and garnish with olive oil. Cover and chill until serving time.   4 cups

*Available in supermarkets or health food stores.

Pickled Kelp

Surprise your guests with this unique condiment. Bull-whip kelp should be harvested when it is young, between June and August. The hollow stalk should snap crisply when bent in two. These are similar to watermelon pickles.

4 pounds bull-whip kelp	3½ cups sugar
1 cup canning salt (non-iodized)	2 cups white vinegar
2 gallons cold water	½ teaspoon oil of cloves*
½ teaspoon alum	½ teaspoon oil of cinnamon*
2 quarts cold water	Green food coloring (optional)

1. Split kelp and cut into 12-inch strips. Wash and peel its dark surface with a vegetable peeler, as you would a cucumber.

2. In a large enamel or stainless steel canner, dissolve salt in 2 gallons of water. Add kelp and soak 2 hours, making sure to keep kelp covered with brine. Drain and rinse.

3. Cut kelp into 1x2-inch strips. In rinsed canner, dissolve alum in 2 quarts cold water. Add kelp and soak 15 minutes, making sure to keep kelp covered with alum solution. Drain, rinse and return to canner.

4. Add enough water to cover kelp; boil until kelp can be pierced with a fork; drain.

5. In a medium saucepan, boil sugar, vinegar and oils for 2 minutes. Pour over cooked kelp. Let stand overnight in a covered stainless steel pan.

6. In the morning, drain off syrup into medium saucepan and reheat to boiling. Pour over kelp again and let stand 24 hours more.

7. On third morning, heat both kelp and syrup to boiling. Pack in sterile canning jars and seal while hot. Add food coloring, if you want pickles a bright green. Store in a cool, dark room. Use within 2 months, as kelp does not keep.

3 pints

*Available in health food stores. If you cannot find the oils, use whole spices tied in a cheesecloth bag. Discard bag before canning.

Pickled Salmon

This takes some time but is well worth the effort. We recommend sockeye, but other species may be used. Don't miss sampling the onions.

    8 cups rocks salt
    2 cups water
    2 pounds unskinned salmon fillet, boned
    4 medium onions, sliced and rings separated
    3 cups brown sugar
    1 (3-ounce) jar pickling spice
    2 quarts cider vinegar

1. To salt cure salmon: In a crock or jar, layer the salmon with salt. Pour in water. Refrigerate for 1 week. The salt cure is necessary to prevent "mushy" salmon.

2. After 1 week, freshen salmon: Discarding brine, rinse salmon in cold water and return to crock. Cover with cold water and refrigerate for 24 hours.

3. Drain salmon in a colander. Cut salmon into 1-inch chunks, leaving the skin on. In wide mouth quart jars, layer salmon, then onion rings, then brown sugar and pickling spice. Repeat layering until jar is full. If you do not want your salmon "hot," remove some of the red peppers from pickling spice.

4. When jars are full, fill with vinegar. Cover and refrigerate for 1 week before eating. Salmon will keep 6 weeks in the refrigerator.   3 quarts

Sautéed Shrimp and Artichokes

A hard-to-beat combination for a hot appetizer on a cold winter night.

    1 pound raw medium-size shrimp, peeled, rinsed, deveined
    2 tablespoons butter
    2 tablespoons olive oil
    2 cloves garlic, minced
    2 shallots or green onions, minced
    1/2 pound raw button mushrooms
    1 (16-ounce) can artichoke hearts, drained and sliced in half

2 tablespoons lemon juice
½ teaspoon dried oregano
½ teaspoon salt
Freshly ground pepper, to taste

1. In a frying pan, over medium heat, melt butter and olive oil. Add garlic and shallots; sauté until softened.

2. Add shrimp and mushrooms and sauté until shrimp is pink and whole mushrooms are heated through. Add artichokes, lemon juice and oregano; heat through. Salt and pepper to taste.

3. Keep hot over warmer; serve with toothpicks and napkins.

8 servings.

Bud's Dilly Beans

These are a favorite appetizer and also delicious in a Bloody Mary. Can in late August when beans are garden fresh.

2 pounds green beans
1 teaspoon cayenne pepper
4 cloves garlic, peeled and cut in half
4 heads of fresh dill weed

2½ cups water
2½ cups vinegar
¼ cup canning salt (non-iodized)

1. In 4 sterile pint jars, carefully pack beans 1-inch from top, lengthwise. To each jar, add ¼ teaspoon cayenne, 1 clove garlic and 1 head of dill.

2. In a large saucepan, bring to a boil water, vinegar and salt. Pour into each jar to cover beans.

3. To can beans, tighten sterile canning lids on jars. Immerse jars in hot water bath for 10 minutes. Let cool and store in a cool, dark room. For the full flavor to develop, wait one month before eating.   4 pints

Rita's Antipasto

This is an exceptional antipasto—a favorite at Guemes Island gatherings. It should be canned in the fall when peppers are at their best and reasonably priced. Plan to prepare this with a friend and share the wealth.

40 green bell peppers, washed and seeded
$\frac{1}{2}$ cup canning salt (non-iodized)
$1\frac{1}{2}$ cups vegetable oil
$2\frac{1}{2}$ cups cider vinegar
3 (6-ounce) cans tomato paste
3 (6-ounce) cans water
3 (2-ounce) cans anchovies, chopped (discard oil)
3 tablespoons pickling spices, tied in a cheesecloth bag
2 tablespoons sugar
1 teaspoon allspice
4 ($6\frac{1}{2}$-ounce) cans tuna, drained and separated
1 pound button mushrooms, cleaned and sliced
1 (16-ounce) can small tender onions, including liquid
1 (16-ounce) jar pimiento green olives, including liquid
2 heads cauliflower, separated into flowerets and steamed tender-crisp

1. Cut peppers into 1-inch squares and place in a large enamel or stainless steel canner. Sprinkle with salt; cover and let stand in a cool room overnight.

2. Next morning, in a large kettle, mix together next 6 ingredients and simmer 15 minutes.

3. Drain peppers, discarding liquid, and add them to tomato sauce. Simmer until tender, about 40 minutes. Stir to prevent burning.

4. Add remaining ingredients and heat through, again stirring to avoid burning. Pour antipasto into sterilized canning jars and close tightly with sterilized lids.

5. Preheat oven to 300°. Place sealed jars in a large roasting pan; jars should not touch. Pour hot water to halfway level on jars. Place roasting pan in oven and process for 15-20 minutes.

6. Remove from oven and place jars on towels in a draft-free room to seal and cool. Store in a cool, dark room. Serve in a bowl with crackers.

20 pints

Salmon Salad with Lemon-Dill Dressing

This island favorite makes a satisfying luncheon or light supper salad. It is a delicious way to use left-over salmon.

LEMON-DILL DRESSING (see below)
6 ounces shell-shaped pasta
1 cup frozen peas
2 cups cooked salmon, broken into chunks
3/4 cup chopped celery
1/2 green pepper, diced
1/4 cup chopped green onion
1/3 cup sliced green olives with pimiento
2 hard cooked eggs, sliced
Salt and pepper, to taste
Lettuce
Lemon wedges

1. Prepare Lemon-Dill Dressing and set aside.

2. In a large pot, cook pasta al dente, according to package directions. Drain, return to pot and toss with Lemon-Dill Dressing; set aside.

3. Place peas in colander and rinse with warm water until peas separate. Drain and pour over pasta. Add next 6 ingredients. Toss gently, salt and pepper to taste. Cover and chill for at least 3 hours.

4. To serve, line 4 plates with crisp greens, spoon on salmon salad and garnish with lemon wedges.   8 servings

LEMON-DILL DRESSING

3/4 cup mayonnaise
1/4 cup fresh lemon juice
2 teaspoons Dijon mustard
1 teaspoon dried dill weed
Salt and pepper, to taste

In a small bowl, combine dressing ingredients.   1 cup

Pasta Salad

Feel free to vary the vegetables with those of your choice. With our Herb Dressing, it cannot fail. The salad will keep in the refrigerator for several days.

HERB DRESSING (see below)
8 ounces rotini spiral pasta
2 tablespoons PESTO SAUCE (optional)
1 head broccoli ($\frac{1}{2}$ pound) cut into flowerets, stalk peeled and thinly sliced
$\frac{1}{2}$ head cauliflower, cut into flowerets
1 medium carrot, thinly sliced
1 stalk celery, thinly sliced
$\frac{1}{2}$ sweet red pepper, seeded and thinly sliced
4 green onions, thinly sliced
$\frac{1}{2}$ cup sliced Greek or ripe olives
2 tablespoons minced parsley
$\frac{1}{4}$ cup freshly grated Parmesan cheese

1. Prepare Herb Dressing and set aside.
2. In a large pot, cook pasta al dente according to package directions. Drain, return pasta to pot and toss with Herb Dressing and Pesto.
3. Add remaining ingredients to pasta and toss to coat. Cover and chill 3 hours or longer to blend flavors.   8 servings

HERB DRESSING

1 tablespoon lemon juice
3 tablespoons red wine vinegar
$\frac{1}{4}$ teaspoon dried oregano
$\frac{1}{4}$ teaspoon dried basil
1 teaspoon salt
$\frac{1}{8}$ teaspoon ground pepper
$\frac{1}{2}$ cup olive oil

In a small bowl, combine all ingredients except oil. Add oil gradually, blending with a whisk. $\frac{3}{4}$ cup

Tortellini Salad

This popular pasta satisfies hearty appetites.

>   1 pound cheese stuffed tortellini
>   2 tablespoons olive oil
>   1 head broccoli (½ pound) cut into flowerets, stems peeled and sliced
>   1 cup julienned green beans
>   1 (6-ounce) jar marinated artichoke hearts, drained and sliced
>   ½ bell pepper, seeded and thinly sliced
>   4 green onions, sliced with some green
>   ½ cup sliced Greek or ripe olives
>   ¼ cup chopped fresh parsley
>   ⅓ cup Parmesan cheese
>   DIJON VINAIGRETTE (see page 64)

1. Cook tortellini in boiling salted water, following package instructions. Drain and set aside in large bowl. Toss with oil to prevent sticking.

2. Steam broccoli and beans separately, until tender-crisp and bright green. Immediately remove from heat and immerse in cold water. Drain and add to tortellini.

3. Add artichokes, bell pepper, onion, olives, parsley and Parmesan cheese.

4. Prepare Dijon Vinaigrette and pour over salad; toss gently. Chill for at least 4 hours before serving. This will keep in the refrigerator for 4 days.

4 servings

Mushroom Salad

This memorable salad is a special first course for an elegant dinner. Prepare it early in the day or the night before.

HERB MARINADE (see below)
1 pound fresh mushrooms, quartered
1 medium red onion, thinly sliced with rings separated
CREAMY MUSTARD DRESSING (see below)
Romaine or Buttercrunch lettuce leaves
1/2 pound cooked small shrimp (optional)

1. Prepare Herb Marinade and add mushrooms and onions. Cover and chill approximately 8 hours.
2. Prepare Creamy Mustard Dressing and set aside.
3. Drain mushrooms and onions and place in a large bowl. Discard Herb Marinade. Toss mushrooms and onions with Creamy Mustard Dressing.
4. Spoon over bed of lettuce. Garnish with shrimp, if desired, and serve immediately.   6 servings

HERB MARINADE

1/2 cup dry white wine
1 tablespoon lemon juice
1 tablespoon olive oil
1/4 teaspoon dried basil

1/4 teaspoon dried oregano
1/4 teaspoon salt
1/8 teaspoon freshly ground pepper

In a medium bowl, whisk together above ingredients.

CREAMY MUSTARD DRESSING

1 egg yolk
2 tablespoons red wine vinegar
2 tablespoons fresh lemon juice
1 tablespoon Dijon mustard
1 clove garlic, minced

1/4 teaspoon salt
1/8 teaspoon freshly ground pepper
1/3 cup olive oil
1/3 cup salad oil

In a medium bowl, whisk together all ingredients except oils. Add oils gradually, blending with whisk. Cover and chill until ready to use.

3/4 cup

Rice and Artichoke Salad

A festive salad to serve at your next salmon barbecue.

2 cups uncooked long-grain rice
4 cups CHICKEN STOCK
2 cups cooked shrimp (optional)
1 (6-ounce) jar marinated artichoke hearts, drained and sliced
6 green onions including tops, sliced
1 cup sliced celery
½ cup chopped green pepper
¼ cup sliced green pimiento olives
½ cup mayonnaise
½ cup sour cream or yogurt
2 tablespoons lemon juice
1 tablespoon curry
¾ teaspoon salt
Freshly ground pepper
Lettuce

1. In medium pan, cook rice in chicken stock, according to package instructions. Remove rice to large bowl and fluff to cool. Add next 6 ingredients.

2. In a small bowl, combine mayonnaise, sour cream, lemon, curry and salt and pepper. Pour over rice mixture; toss lightly. Cover and chill at least 1 hour.

3. Serve on a bed of lettuce.   6 servings

Marinated Zucchini Salad

Make this flavorful salad in August when zucchini is plentiful. The Red Pepper Marinade provides a delightful spicy flavor.

RED PEPPER MARINADE (see below)
4 medium zucchini, diced into 1/2-inch chunks
1 cup sliced celery
1/2 cup diced red sweet pepper
1/2 cup diced green pepper
1/4 cup thinly sliced red onion
1/2 cup sliced ripe olives
1/4 cup sliced green olives

1. Prepare Red Pepper Marinade and set aside.
2. In large bowl, combine all salad ingredients. Pour marinade over salad and toss lightly. Cover and chill for at least 6 hours before serving.

6 servings

RED PEPPER MARINADE

1/4 cup red wine vinegar
1/4 cup chopped fresh parsley
1 teaspoon dried basil
1 teaspoon dried oregano
1/4-1/2 teaspoon dried red peppers
1 teaspoon salt
1/2 teaspoon freshly ground pepper
2/3 cup olive oil

In a small bowl, combine all ingredients except oil. Add olive oil gradually, blending with a whisk.

Niçoise Salad

This is a wonderful main-dish salad. It can be prepared the day before and tossed at serving time. Serve with crusty French bread and a dry white wine.

   3 medium new potatoes
   NIÇOISE DRESSING (recipe follows)
   4 ounces green beans
   ¼ cup mayonnaise
   ¼ cup sour cream
   ½ teaspoon dried dill weed
   ¼ cup green pepper, thinly sliced
   1 (6½-ounce) can tuna, drained
   1 bunch Romaine, Buttercrunch, or Leaf lettuce, torn into bite-size pieces
   2 hard-cooked eggs
   ¼ cup alfalfa sprouts
   Salt and coarsely ground pepper, to taste

1. Cut potatoes in half and cook in small amount of boiling water until tender when pierced, about 15 minutes. Remove from heat, drain and peel. Cut into ¼-inch slices and place in a salad bowl.

2. While potatoes are cooking, prepare Nicoise Dressing. Pour over warm potatoes and set aside.

3. Steam beans until bright green and tender, about 9 minutes. Immediately remove from heat and immerse in ice water to prevent further cooking. Drain and set aside.

4. In a small bowl, combine mayonnaise, sour cream and dill weed. Pour over potatoes and toss to coat. Top potatoes with green pepper, tuna, and green beans. Add lettuce and top with egg slices and sprouts. Do not toss until serving time.

5. Cover and chill overnight, if desired, or toss and serve immediately. Salt and pepper to taste.   4 servings

NIÇOISE DRESSING

¼ cup wine vinegar
1 tablespoon Dijon mustard
4 anchovy fillets, drained and minced
1 clove garlic, minced
2 green onions, thinly sliced
Freshly ground pepper, to taste
½ cup vegetable oil

In a small bowl, combine all ingredients, except oil. Add oil gradually, blending with a whisk.   ¾ cup

Scandinavian Cucumbers

Crisp and refreshing on a hot summer day.

4 medium cucumbers, thinly sliced
½ cup sour cream
¼ cup yogurt
2 tablespoons tarragon vinegar
½ teaspoon dried dill weed or 2 teaspoons dill sprigs
2 tablespoons finely chopped parsley
1 teaspoon sugar
¼ cup green onions, minced
1 teaspoon salt
⅛ teaspoon freshly ground pepper

1. Place cucumbers on paper towels to absorb excess moisture.
2. In a medium bowl, stir together all ingredients, except cucumbers and onion. Gently fold in cucumbers and onion. Cover and chill at least 2 hours.

4-6 servings

Janice's Potato Salad

A delicious salad with garden-fresh potatoes.

5 medium new potatoes
1½ cups mayonnaise
1 tablespoon Dijon mustard
1 tablespoon red wine vinegar
1 tablespoon capers
1 teaspoon dried dill weed
Salt and freshly ground pepper, to taste
3 hard-cooked eggs, sliced
2 celery stalks, diced
4 green onions, sliced without tops
½ cup coarsely chopped dill pickle

1. Wash potatoes and cut in half. In a large pot, cook potatoes in a small amount of boiling water until tender when pierced, about 15 minutes. Remove from heat, drain and peel. Cut into ¼-inch slices and place in a salad bowl.

2. While potatoes are cooking, in a small bowl, combine mayonnaise, mustard, vinegar, capers, dill weed, salt and pepper. Pour mayonnaise mixture over cooled potatoes.

3. Add remaining ingredients and toss gently to blend. Adjust seasonings as desired. Cover and chill for at least 1 hour.   6-8 servings

Marinated Beef and Mushroom Salad

Take this hearty main-dish salad on your next picnic for a sumptuous feast.

Marinade
3 tablespoons soy sauce
1/4 cup red wine vinegar
1/4 cup vegetable oil
1/4 cup water
2 cloves garlic, finely chopped
4 drops Tabasco sauce
Freshly ground pepper
Salad Ingredients
2 pounds sirloin or flank steak
4 medium potatoes
2 tablespoons butter or margarine
1/2 pound fresh mushrooms, washed and sliced
1/3 medium green pepper, julienned
1/4 small purple onion, sliced into rings and separated
2 small tomatoes, cut into wedges and seeded
2 tablespoons chopped fresh parsley
DIJON VINAIGRETTE (see page 64)
Leaf lettuce, washed and patted dry

1. To make marinade, combine first 7 ingredients in a small bowl. Place steak in shallow baking dish; pour marinade over meat. Cover and refrigerate for approximately 3 hours.

2. Remove steak from marinade and place on broiling pan. Broil steak 2 inches from heat, until medium rare, about 5 minutes each side. Cool, slice into 1/4-inch strips. Set aside in a large salad bowl.

3. Place halved potatoes in a medium saucepan and add enough salted water to cover. Bring to boil, reduce heat and continue cooking until tender but not mushy, about 10 minutes. Drain and cool. Peel and cut into large chunks; add to steak strips.

4. While potatoes are cooking, melt butter in a small frying pan, over medium heat. Sauté mushrooms until barely tender. Using a slotted spoon, remove mushrooms and add to steak.

5. Add green pepper, onion, tomatoes and parsley to steak.

6. Prepare Dijon Vinaigrette. Pour desired amount over steak and vegetables; toss lightly. Serve on a bed of lettuce leaves.   6 servings

Asparagus Salad with Dijon Vinaigrette

This salad is a perfect accompaniment to a spring leg of lamb.

   1 pound asparagus (about 20 spears) tough ends trimmed
   ½ cup DIJON VINAIGRETTE (see page 64)
   1 hard-cooked egg, finely chopped

   1. In a large pan, cook the asparagus, uncovered, in boiling water until fork-tender, about 6-8 minutes. Do not overcook. Rinse in cold water and drain. Place asparagus on a platter; cover and chill.
   2. Prepare Dijon Vinaigrette; cover and chill.
   3. An hour before serving, crumble egg over asparagus. Top with the vinaigrette. Cover and chill until ready to serve.   4 servings

Gingered Carrot Salad

The ginger adds a surprising flavor to this tasty year-round salad.

   ¼ cup salad oil
   ½ tablespoon fresh lemon juice
   ½ teaspoon sugar
   ½ teaspoon salt
   ¼ teaspoon ginger or ½ teaspoon grated fresh ginger root
   4 large sweet carrots, shredded
   ¼ cup raisins
   ¼ cup coarsely chopped walnuts

   1. In a medium bowl, whisk together oil, lemon juice, sugar, salt and ginger. Stir in carrots, and raisins.
   2. Cover and chill salad for 2 hours. Before serving gently stir in walnuts.   4 servings

Curried Chicken Salad

The curry gives a Far Eastern touch to this popular Pacific Northwest salad.

2 whole chicken breasts (4 halves) split and skinned
1 stalk celery, halved
½ pound bacon, finely sliced
2 tablespoons butter
1 cup sliced almonds
2-3 red crisp apples, cored and diced
2 tablespoons fresh lemon juice
½ cup chopped celery
1½ cups mayonnaise
2 tablespoons curry powder
Salt and pepper, to taste
1 head Bibb lettuce
Chutney

1. In a medium stock pot, boil chicken and celery stalk in enough salted water to cover, about 30-40 minutes. Transfer chicken to a bowl; cover and chill at least 1 hour. Reserve chicken broth for another use.

2. Fry bacon until crisp; drain on paper towel. Discard bacon grease from frying pan. Melt butter and sauté almonds until lightly toasted; set aside.

3. In large bowl, combine diced apples and lemon juice (to prevent browning). Add chopped celery and almonds.

4. In a small bowl, thoroughly mix mayonnaise and curry; set aside.

5. Bone cold chicken and dice; add chicken to apple mixture. Toss gently with curried mayonnaise. Salt and pepper to taste.

6. To serve, line eight plates with lettuce, spoon on curried chicken. Garnish with bacon. Serve chutney as a condiment.   8 servings

August Harvest Vinaigrette

Fresh garden produce creates a tasty salad when teamed with our Basil Vinaigrette.

    4 small tender zucchini, cut into 2-inch chunks
    BASIL VINAIGRETTE (see below)
    2 medium tomatoes, peeled and quartered
    1 large cucumber, peeled and sliced
    Parmesan cheese

1. In a large pot, steam zucchini until crisp-tender, about 6 minutes. Remove from heat and drain; set aside to cool in a large bowl.

2. Prepare Basil Vinaigrette and set aside.

3. Add tomatoes and cucumber to zucchini. Pour dressing over vegetables and toss gently.

4. Transfer salad to serving bowl. Garnish with Parmesan cheese.

4 servings

BASIL VINAIGRETTE

    2 tablespoons red wine vinegar
    1 tablespoon lemon juice
    1 tablespoon chopped fresh parsley
    1 clove garlic, minced
    3 teaspoons fresh minced basil
    1/2 teaspoon salt
    1/4 teaspoon coarsely ground pepper
    2 tablespoons olive oil
    1/3 cup salad oil

In a small bowl, combine all ingredients, except oils. Add oils gradually, blending with a whisk.

1/2 cup

New Potato Salad

This is a tasty alternative to a traditional potato salad.

2 pounds new potatoes
6 slices bacon, diced and cooked crisp, drained
4 hard cooked eggs
1/4 cup thinly sliced green onions
1/4 cup sliced black olives
1/2 cup sliced radishes (optional)
1/3 cup chopped fresh parsley
TARRAGON-MUSTARD DRESSING (see below)

1. Wash potatoes and place in large saucepan with enough salted water to cover. Bring to a boil; reduce heat and simmer about 15 minutes or until tender. Drain, cool and slice into 1/4-inch rounds.

2. Crumble bacon, slice eggs and add to potatoes. Add green onions, olives, radishes and parsley; toss gently.

3. Prepare Tarragon-Mustard Dressing. Pour dressing over salad and toss to coat potatoes evenly. Transfer to serving bowl; cover and refrigerate approximately 3 hours before serving.   6 servings

TARRAGON-MUSTARD DRESSING

1/4 cup tarragon wine vinegar
1 tablespoon Dijon mustard
1/2 teaspoon dried tarragon
Salt and freshly ground pepper, to taste
1/2 cup olive oil or salad oil

In a small bowl, combine all ingredients except oil. Slowly add oil whisking to blend.   3/4 cup

Vegetable Bean Salad

A versatile salad that can be made ahead and kept in the refrigerator for up to a week.

  ½ head cauliflower, cut into flowerets
  1 bunch (½ pound) broccoli, separated into flowerets, stems peeled and sliced
  2 carrots, sliced
  TARRAGON VINAIGRETTE (recipe follows)
  2 stalks celery, sliced
  6 green onions, sliced
  ¼ cup chopped fresh parsley
  1 (16-ounce) can garbanzo beans, drained
  1 (16-ounce) can kidney beans, drained
  1 (8-ounce) can green beans, drained
  1 (8-ounce) can yellow wax beans, drained
  1 cup sliced Greek or ripe olives
  1 red pepper, finely chopped
  1 (6-ounce) jar marinated artichoke hearts, drained and quartered
  1 bay leaf

1. In a saucepan, steam cauliflower, broccoli and carrots until tender-crisp. Drain and transfer to a large bowl.

2. Prepare Tarragon Vinaigrette and pour over warm vegetables.

3. Add all remaining salad ingredients and toss gently. Cover and refrigerate at least 1 day. Before serving, remove bay leaf.   12 servings

TARRAGON VINAIGRETTE

  ⅔ cup balsamic or tarragon vinegar
  ¼ cup fresh lemon juice
  1 teaspoon dried tarragon
  1 teaspoon dried basil
  ½ teaspoon dried marjoram
  1 tablespoon sugar
  Salt and pepper, to taste
  1 cup olive oil or vegetable oil

In a small bowl, combine all ingredients, except oil. Add oil gradually, blending with a whisk.   1 cup

Vegetable Vinaigrette

This healthful salad is popular at Shaw Island gatherings.

½ head cauliflower, cut into flowerets
2 bunches broccoli (about 1 pound) cut into flowerets, stalks peeled and sliced
    diagonally
3 carrots, peeled and sliced diagonally
OREGANO VINAIGRETTE (see below)
1 (16-ounce) can ripe olives, drained
½ pound large mushrooms, halved
2 tablespoons Parmesan cheese

1. In a large pot, steam cauliflower, broccoli and carrots until tender-crisp, about 5 minutes. Drain and set aside in a large bowl.

2. While vegetables are steaming, prepare Oregano Vinaigrette; pour over warm vegetables. Add olives and mushrooms and toss.

3. Sprinkle vegetables with Parmesan and toss gently. Cover and chill for 4 hours or longer. This will keep for a week in the refrigerator. To serve, remove vegetables with a slotted spoon and place in a serving dish. Serve with additional Parmesan cheese, if desired.   8 servings

OREGANO VINAIGRETTE

½ cup white wine vinegar
2 tablespoons fresh lemon juice
1 tablespoon chopped fresh parsley
1 teaspoon dried oregano
Salt and freshly ground pepper, to taste
¾ cup salad or olive oil

In a small bowl, combine all ingredients, except oil. Add oil gradually, blending with a whisk.   1½ cups

Shrimp and Vegetable Salad

Crisp raw vegetables and water chestnuts make this a year-round favorite.

 1 small head cauliflower, cut into flowerets
 2 bunches broccoli (about 1 pound) cut into flowerets, stalks peeled and sliced
 1 (8½-ounce) can water chestnuts, drained and thinly sliced
 ½ cup thinly sliced celery
 ⅓ cup finely chopped green onions
 2 cups cooked small shrimp
 Salt and pepper, to taste
 DRESSING (see below)

1. In a large bowl, combine all salad ingredients.

2. Prepare Dressing and pour over salad and toss gently. Salt and pepper to taste. Cover and chill at least 3 hours before serving.   8 servings

DRESSING

 1 cup mayonnaise
 2 tablespoons lemon juice
 1 teaspoon dried dill weed
 4 teaspoons red wine vinegar
 2 teaspoons Dijon mustard

In a small bowl, mix together dressing ingredients.   1 cup

Greek Tomato Salad

Prepare this colorful salad a day in advance, if desired. Its unique flavor complements simple entrees, such as barbecued salmon.

> 6 medium tomatoes, sliced
> 1/4 pound feta cheese, crumbled
> 1 small red onion, thinly sliced and rings separated
> 1/2 cup sliced Greek or ripe olives
> 2 cucumbers, peeled and diced
> 1/2 green pepper, diced
> GREEK DRESSING (see below)
> Lettuce leaves

1. In a 13x9-inch dish, layer sliced tomatoes, feta cheese, onion, olives, cucumber and green pepper.
2. Prepare Greek Dressing and pour over the salad. Cover and chill at least 2 hours.
3. To serve, line a large platter with lettuce leaves. Carefully spoon chilled salad over lettuce.   8 servings

GREEK DRESSING

> 1/3 cup red wine vinegar
> 2 tablespoons chopped fresh parsley
> 1 clove garlic, minced
> 4 teaspoons sugar
> 1/2 teaspoon dried basil
> 1/4 teaspoon salt
> 1/4 teaspoon coarsely ground pepper
> 1/2 cup olive oil

In a small bowl, combine all ingredients, except oil. Add oil gradually, beating with a whisk until blended.   1 cup

Napa Slaw with Creamy Dill Dressing

If this is made ahead, do not blend dressing with cabbage until serving time.

CREAMY DILL DRESSING (see below)
1 medium head Chinese cabbage, cut into bite-size pieces
½ cup thinly sliced mild radishes (optional)
1 avocado, sliced

1. Prepare Creamy Dill Dressing and set aside.
2. In a large bowl, combine cabbage and radishes. Pour dressing over salad ingredients and gently toss.
3. Garnish with avocado and serve immediately.   6 servings

CREAMY DILL DRESSING

¾ cup mayonnaise
¼ cup buttermilk
1 tablespoon red wine vinegar
1 teaspoon fresh lemon juice
2 teaspoons soy sauce
½ teaspoon dried dill weed
Salt and pepper, to taste

In a small bowl, combine all dressing ingredients.   1 cup

Coleslaw with Shrimp

This is a San Juan variation of traditional coleslaw.

 4 cups finely shredded cabbage
 2 tablespoons sliced green onions
 1 cup chopped cucumber
 1 cup cooked small shrimp, deveined, washed and drained
 DRESSING (see below)
 1 avocado
 ½ tablespoon fresh lemon juice
 Dill weed

1. In a large bowl, combine the cabbage, onion and cucumber. Fold in shrimp.

2. Prepare Dressing and toss with salad ingredients. Peel and slice avocado; arrange on top of salad. Squeeze lemon juice over avocado to prevent darkening. Sprinkle with dill weed and serve immediately.   6 servings

DRESSING

 1 cup mayonnaise
 2 tablespoons lemon juice
 ½ teaspoon salt or celery salt
 1 teaspoon dried dill weed
 Dash paprika

In a small bowl, combine ingredients and mix until smooth.   1 cup

Citrus and Cashew Green Salad

Serve this refreshing salad in early winter when grapefruit is sweet.

DRESSING (see below)
1 head Bibb or leaf lettuce, washed and drained
1 orange, peeled and sectioned with membranes removed
1/2 sweet grapefruit, peeled and sectioned with membranes removed
1 avocado, peeled and sliced
1/3 cup cashews

1. Prepare Dressing and set aside.
2. Tear lettuce leaves into bite-size pieces and place in a salad bowl. Cut orange and grapefruit sections in half and add to lettuce.
3. Pour dressing over salad and toss gently. Garnish with sliced avocado and cashews. Serve immediately.   6 servings

DRESSING

3 tablespoons red wine vinegar
1 tablespoon fresh lemon juice
1/2 teaspoon sugar
1/4 teaspoon dry mustard
Salt and freshly ground pepper, to taste
1/3 cup vegetable oil

In a small bowl, combine all ingredients, except oil. Add oil gradually, blending with a whisk.   1/2 cup

Spinach Caesar Salad

A classic Caesar Dressing served on tender spinach greens.

GARLIC CROUTONS (see below)
1 large bunch spinach, stemmed and washed
1 clove garlic
1 egg
CAESAR DRESSING (recipe follows)
1/4 cup grated Parmesan cheese

1. Prepare Garlic Croutons and set aside.
2. Tear spinach into bite-size pieces. Rub inside of salad bowl with garlic clove; discard garlic. Place spinach in bowl. Cover and chill.
3. In a small pan, cover egg with warm water and boil for 1 minute. Remove immediately from heat and cool in cold water; set aside.
4. Prepare Caesar Dressing and pour over spinach. Break the coddled egg over salad. Sprinkle with Parmesan cheese and croutons. Toss gently to blend. Serve immediately.   6 servings

GARLIC CROUTONS

2 tablespoons butter or margarine, at room temperature
5 slices bread
1/4 teaspoon garlic powder
1 tablespoon grated Parmesan cheese

1. Preheat over to 375°. Butter bread and sprinkle with garlic powder. Cut bread into 1/2-inch cubes and place on baking sheet.
2. Bake for 20-30 minutes until golden brown, stirring occasionally. Remove from oven and sprinkle with grated Parmesan cheese. Store in covered jar in refrigerator for up to 6 weeks.   4 cups

CAESAR DRESSING

2 tablespoons wine vinegar
1/4 cup fresh lemon juice
Dash Worcestershire sauce
2-3 anchovy fillets, chopped
Salt and freshly ground pepper, to taste
1/3 cup olive oil

In a small bowl, combine all ingredients, except oil. Add oil gradually, blending with a whisk. Correct seasonings to taste.   2/3 cup

Spinach Salad with Bacon and Apple

A perfect accompaniment for a Christmas prime rib.

1 pound fresh spinach, stemmed and washed
DRESSING (see below)
5 slices bacon, sliced
⅓ cup sliced almonds
3 green onions including tops, thinly sliced
1 crisp Red Delicious apple

1. Tear spinach into bite-size pieces and place in a serving bowl; cover and chill.

2. Prepare Dressing and set aside.

3. In a medium frying pan, over medium heat, sauté the bacon until crisp. Drain on paper towels.

4. Discard all but 1 teaspoon bacon drippings and toast the almonds until golden. Remove from pan and drain.

5. Remove spinach bowl from refrigerator; add bacon, almonds and green onion. Core and dice apple; add to salad bowl. Pour Dressing over salad and toss gently. Serve immediately.   6 servings

DRESSING

3 tablespoons tarragon wine vinegar
1 teaspoon sugar
½ teaspoon dry mustard
Salt and freshly ground pepper, to taste
¼ cup vegetable oil

In a small bowl, combine all ingredients, except oil. Add oil gradually, blending with a whisk.   ¼ cup

Spinach Salad with Pine Nut Dressing

La Famiglia Ristorante on Orcas Island features local produce and seafood in their daily chef's specials. Patty Brogi shared this popular Italian salad with us.

1 bunch spinach, stemmed and washed
3/4 cup pine nuts
1/2 teaspoon tarragon leaves
1/4 teaspoon grated lemon peel
1/8 teaspoon ground nutmeg
1/3 cup wine vinegar
1/2 teaspoon salt
1/2 cup olive oil
Ground nutmeg

1. Tear spinach into bite-size pieces; chill until crisp.

2. In a shallow pan, place pine nuts in a single layer. Bake at 350° for 5 minutes or until golden. Stir occasionally.

3. Prepare dressing in a small bowl, combining tarragon, lemon peel, nutmeg, vinegar and salt. Gradually add oil, whisking constantly until thick. Mix well before using.

4. Place spinach on salad plates and sprinkle with pine nuts. Spoon dressing over greens and sprinkle lightly with nutmeg.   6-8 servings

Fruit Salad

The ingredients for this salad are best if prepared just before serving. Choose fruits that are fresh and in season. Apples, pears and peaches need a squeeze of lemon juice if there is no citrus fruit in the salad. Berries and bananas should be sliced on top, so that they will not mush when tossed. We have included two dressings which are quite different; choose your own favorite.

POPPY SEED or HONEY YOGURT DRESSING (see below)
8 cups assorted fruit: oranges, apples, pears, peaches, melons, grapefruit, pineapple, kiwi, grapes, bananas and berries
Lettuce
½ cup coconut (optional)
Mint leaves (optional)

1. Prepare Poppy Seed or Honey Yogurt Dressing. Cover and chill.
2. Prepare fruit and place in a salad bowl lined with lettuce; add coconut, if desired.
3. Pour dressing over fruit salad; gently toss. Garnish with mint leaves, if desired.   8 servings

POPPY SEED DRESSING

¼ cup granulated sugar
1 tablespoon yellow onion, grated
1 teaspoon dry mustard
⅓ cup red wine vinegar

½ teaspoon salt
1 tablespoon poppy seeds
1 cup vegetable oil

In a small bowl, combine first 6 ingredients. Add oil gradually, blending with a whisk.   1½ cups

HONEY YOGURT DRESSING

2 cups plain or flavored yogurt
2 teaspoons fresh lemon juice
Honey, to taste

In a small bowl, combine yogurt and lemon juice. Add honey to taste.

2 cups

Sauerkraut Salad

This colorful salad is terrific to take on a picnic or serve at a barbecue.

½ cup sugar
½ cup vegetable oil
⅓ cup cider vinegar
½ cup chopped green onions
1 cup diced green pepper or ½ cup green and ½ cup red pepper
1 cup chopped celery
2 teaspoons celery seeds
4 cups fresh sauerkraut, drained

1. In a large bowl, combine sugar, salad oil and vinegar. Stir until sugar dissolves.

2. Add remaining ingredients and toss to coat sauerkraut. Cover and refrigerate overnight.   8 servings

Eggplant Garden Salad

Prepare early in the day to fully blend the flavors of this surprisingly delectable salad.

2 medium eggplants
3 medium tomatoes, seeded and diced
1/4 cup chopped sweet green pepper
3 green onions, finely chopped
1/2 cup peeled and diced cucumber
1/4 cup chopped fresh parsley
1/4 cup yogurt or mayonnaise
5 tablespoons fresh lemon juice
1/4 cup olive oil
1/2 teaspoon dried dill weed or 3 sprigs fresh dill
Salt and freshly ground pepper, to taste
Parsley

1. Preheat oven to 375°. Remove stems from eggplants and pierce skins with fork. Bake in a shallow baking dish for 1 hour or until soft. Remove from oven to cool.

2. Peel eggplants and cut into bite-size chunks. Place in a large bowl. Add tomatoes, green pepper, onion, cucumber and parsley.

3. In a small bowl, mix yogurt, lemon juice, olive oil, dill weed, salt and pepper. Spoon over vegetables and gently toss. Cover and chill for at least 1 hour. Garnish with additional parsley.   6-8 servings

Raspberry Vinegar

Use this delightful vinegar in sauces and dressings. It also makes a festive gift in fancy bottles with your own label. Recipe can easily be doubled, if preparing for gifts.

1½ pounds raspberries, fresh or unsugared frozen, mashed
½ cup sugar
Red wine vinegar

1. Place raspberries and sugar in wide-mouthed quart jar. Add enough vinegar to fill jar to the top.
2. Place uncovered jar on a small rack in a deep saucepan. Pour water in saucepan to halfway level on outside of jar. Bring water to a boil over high heat; then reduce heat and simmer for 10 minutes. Remove jar from water bath and let cool.
3. Close jar with lid and shake well. Refrigerate for 3 weeks. Strain through clean cheesecloth to remove pulp; discard pulp.
4. Divide into separate bottles. If mixture seems too thick, add more red wine vinegar. Store tightly closed at room temperature.   1 quart

Raspberry Vinaigrette

5 tablespoons RASPBERRY VINEGAR
1 tablespoon finely chopped shallots
1 tablespoon heavy cream or CREME FRAICHE (see page 212)
Salt and coarsely ground pepper, to taste
½ cup olive oil or vegetable oil

1. In a small bowl, combine all ingredients, except oil.
2. Add oil gradually, beating with a whisk. Add salt and pepper to taste. Cover and chill; blend before using.   ¾ cup

Blue Cheese Vinaigrette

3 tablespoons white wine vinegar
1 clove garlic, finely minced
$\frac{1}{2}$ tablespoon Worcestershire sauce
$\frac{1}{8}$ teaspoon freshly ground pepper
$\frac{2}{3}$ cup olive or salad oil
4 ounces blue cheese, crumbled

1. In a small bowl, combine vinegar, garlic, Worcestershire and pepper.
2. Add oil gradually, blending with a whisk. Stir in crumbled blue cheese. Cover and chill; blend before using.   1 cup

Creamy Blue Cheese Dressing

2 cups sour cream
1 cup mayonnaise
1 clove garlic, finely minced
2 tablespoons lemon juice
4-6 ounces blue cheese, crumbled
1 teaspoon salt
Freshly ground pepper, to taste

In a medium bowl, combine first 5 ingredients. Stir in remaining ingredients. Cover and chill; blend before using. $3\frac{1}{2}$ cups

Creamy Herb Vinaigrette

2 egg yolks
1/4 cup red wine vinegar
2 tablespoons lemon juice
2 cloves garlic, finely minced
1 teaspoon dried basil
1 teaspoon dried thyme
1 teaspoon salt
1/8 teaspoon freshly ground pepper
1 1/2 cups olive or salad oil

1. In a medium bowl, beat eggs until foamy. Add vinegar, lemon, garlic, basil, thyme, salt and pepper.

2. Add oil gradually, blending with a whisk. Cover and chill; blend before using.   1 pint

Mustard Yogurt Dressing

1 cup plain yogurt
1 tablespoon Dijon mustard
1 tablespoon lemon juice or white wine vinegar
2 tablespoons oil
1 tablespoon minced green onion
1 tablespoon chopped fresh parsley
1/2 teaspoon salt
1/8 teaspoon freshly ground pepper

In a small bowl, combine all ingredients. Cover and chill; blend well before using.   1 1/4 cups

Creamy Tarragon Dressing

3 egg yolks
3 tablespoons tarragon vinegar
2 tablespoons Dijon mustard
½ teaspoon dried tarragon
Salt and coarsely ground pepper, to taste
1 cup olive oil
½ cup vegetable oil

1. In a mixing bowl or food processor, combine all ingredients, except oils.
2. Gradually add oils, blending constantly until thick. Cover and chill; blend before using.   2 cups

Champagne Dressing

2 egg yolks
2 teaspoons Dijon or champagne mustard
⅓ cup champagne vinegar
Salt and coarsely ground pepper, to taste
1½ cups vegetable oil

1. In a mixing bowl or food processor, combine egg yolks, mustard, vinegar, salt and pepper.
2. Gradually add oil, blending constantly until thick. Cover and chill; blend before using.   2 cups

Dijon Vinaigrette

¼ cup red wine vinegar
1 tablespoon lemon juice
2 tablespoons Dijon mustard
1 clove garlic, minced (optional)
½ teaspoon salt
¼ teaspoon coarsely ground pepper
¾ cup olive oil

In a small bowl, combine all ingredients, except oil. Add oil gradually, blending with a whisk. Cover and chill; blend before using.   1 cup

Seafood

Peter Capen

Low Tide at False Bay

Broil-Bake Salmon

This recipe gives the flavor of an outdoor barbecued salmon with the ease of cooking indoors.

1 (8-pound) salmon, filleted with backbone removed
¼ cup butter or margarine
3 cloves garlic, minced
¼ cup olive oil
2 tablespoons fresh lemon juice
4 green onions, chopped
3 tablespoons minced fresh parsley
1 teaspoon dried dill weed or 1 tablespoon fresh dill sprigs
½ teaspoon salt
¼ teaspoon freshly ground pepper
Lemon wedges
Parsley sprigs

1. Place salmon fillets skin side down, on a foil-lined baking dish. Turn up edges of foil to form a tray.

2. In a small saucepan, melt butter and sauté garlic about 2 minutes. Add next 7 ingredients and keep warm.

3. Place oven rack in second position from top. Preheat broiler.

4. Spoon butter mixture over fillets. Broil with oven door ajar, approximately 10 minutes or until surface is nicely browned. Do not overcook.

5. Close oven door; set oven controls to bake at 350°. Cook 15 minutes more or until fish flakes when pierced with a fork.

6. Remove from oven and place salmon on a heated platter; garnish with lemon wedges and parsley.   10 servings

Samish Indian Barbecued Salmon

Traditionally coastal Indians wove salmon fillets on ironwood or green alder branches to cook over an open fire. The catching of the first salmon of the season lead to a great spiritual ceremony involving the entire village in the preparation and eating of the fish.

1 (10-pound) fresh salmon, dressed and filleted
½ cup rock salt

1. Lay salmon fillets, skin side down, on heavy foil. Sprinkle with salt and let stand for 45 minutes to 1 hour; rinse with cold water and allow to air dry.

2. Prepare alder wood fire 30 minutes before cooking fish. The fire bed should die down to a bed of hot coals.

3. Place salmon fillets, meat side down, on grill about 12 inches from coals. Do not let the flames flair-up and burn the fish. Cook salmon approximately 20 minutes per side, thickness of fish will determine cooking time. Add more wood as needed to maintain a hot bed of coals. Turn fillets over and cook about 20 minutes more or until fish flakes when tested with a fork.   10 servings

Island Barbecued Salmon

To retain the delicious salmon juices, cover the salmon when barbecuing. If you don't have a covered barbecue, make a foil tent. The fish will cook faster and remain moist.

   1 (5-10 pound) salmon, cut into two fillets
   Salt and pepper
   ½ cup butter or margarine
   4 cloves garlic, minced
   ¼ cup fresh lemon juice
   2 tablespoons minced fresh parsley
   1 teaspoon dried dill weed
   1 lemon, sliced
   1 onion, sliced
   Lemon wedges
   TARTAR SAUCE (see page 108)

   1. Cut a heavy sheet of aluminum foil large enough to turn up edges to form a tray. Place salmon fillets on foil, skin side down. Salt and pepper fillets.
   2. In a small saucepan, melt butter and sauté garlic, about 2 minutes. Add lemon juice, parsley and dill weed; heat through. Keep warm to use for basting salmon.
   3. Place salmon and aluminum tray on pre-heated grill. Baste with half of the butter mixture. Layer onion and lemon slices on fillets. Cover barbecue and cook over slow coals, about 15 minutes. Pour remaining butter mixture over salmon and continue cooking with cover on for about 10 minutes more or until fish flakes when tested with a fork.
   4. Transfer to a serving platter. Serve with lemon wedges and tartar sauce.   6-12 servings

Pan-Braised Salmon

The salmon "hot spots" change depending on tidal current and location of bait fish. Salmon Banks, Cattle Point, Black Rock and Hein Bank in the Straits of Juan de Fuca are generally good places to try. This is a quick entree. The combination of garlic, olive oil and onion with fresh salmon is hard to beat for flavor.

4 salmon fillets (6-8 ounces each, approximately ¾-inch thick)
Garlic seasoning salt
Freshly ground pepper
¼ cup olive oil
1 medium onion, sliced and rings separated
Lemon wedges
Parsley sprigs

1. Dry salmon fillets with paper towel and season with garlic salt and pepper.
2. In a large frying pan, heat oil over medium heat. Add onion rings; sauté until slightly softened. Push onion to side of pan.
3. Add salmon fillets, skin side up; do not crowd. Cook until nicely browned. Turn over and cover. Continue cooking until fish flakes when tested with a fork.
4. Place onion rings on each fillet and serve with lemon wedges and parsley sprigs as garnish.   4 servings

Salmon Pasta

This flavorful dish requires only a small amount of fish. It is especially delicious with smoked salmon from Specialty Seafood on Fidalgo Island.

8 ounces farfalle pasta (bow-ties)
2 tablespoons olive oil
2 tablespoons PESTO SAUCE
2 tablespoons butter
¾ pound fresh salmon fillet, boned, skinned and julienned
¼ cup all-purpose flour
4 green onions, sliced diagonally with some tops
¼ cup dry white wine or dry vermouth
1 cup heavy cream
1 teaspoon capers
½ teaspoon dried dill weed
1 tablespoon minced fresh parsley
Salt and freshly ground pepper, to taste
Lemon wedges

1. In a large pot, cook pasta al dente, according to package directions. Drain, return to pot and toss to coat with 2 tablespoons oil and Pesto Sauce. Cover to keep warm.

2. While pasta is cooking, dust salmon with flour. In a large skillet, heat 2 tablespoons butter over medium high heat. Add salmon and onions; sauté for 3 minutes. Add wine, cream, capers, dill weed and parsley. Simmer to reduce and thicken sauce, about 5 minutes.

3. Add salmon mixture to pasta and toss gently. Salt and pepper to taste. Transfer to a warm serving platter. Garnish with lemon wedges and parsley sprigs. Serve immediately. 4 servings

Poached Salmon with Creamy Herb Sauce

This is a rich yet delicately flavored dish to serve with Rice Pilaf.

½ cup dry white wine
1 onion, sliced
1 celery stalk, sliced
1 tablespoon chopped fresh parsley
6 whole black peppercorns
2 tablespoons lemon juice
1 teaspoon salt
1 bay leaf
4 cups water
4-6 salmon steaks, 1-inch thick
CREAMY HERB SAUCE (recipe follows)
Capers

1. In a large pan, prepare poaching liquid by combining all ingredients except salmon. Bring to a boil and reduce heat; cover and simmer 15 minutes. Remove vegetables with a slotted spoon and discard.

2. Place salmon steaks in a 9x13-inch baking pan. Cover with hot poaching liquid. Cover loosely with foil. Bake at 350° for 15 minutes or until fish flakes when pierced with fork.

3. While salmon is baking, prepare Creamy Herb Sauce.

4. Remove salmon from poaching liquid and place on warmed plates. Spoon sauce over salmon. Garnish with capers. Serve immediately.

4-6 servings

CREAMY HERB SAUCE

¼ cup butter
2 cloves garlic, minced
2 tablespoons finely minced shallots or green onions
2 tablespoons flour
¼ cup dry vermouth or dry white wine
¾ cup heavy cream
1 tablespoon fresh lemon juice
¼ teaspoon dried basil
¼ teaspoon dried thyme
Salt and freshly ground pepper, to taste

1. Melt butter in saucepan. Add garlic and onions; sauté until soft, about 3 minutes. Stir in flour and allow to cook about 2 minutes more.

2. Deglaze pan with vermouth. Add cream, lemon juice, basil, thyme, salt and pepper. Cook and stir until thickened; do not boil. Keep warm.

1¼ cups

Salmon Cakes

These crispy cakes will create a whole new meal from your leftover salmon.

4 eggs
2 cups cooked salmon, flaked
1 cup chopped onion
1 cup chopped fresh parsley
$1/2$ cup cracker crumbs
1 tablespoon lemon juice
2 teaspoons dried oregano
$1/4$ teaspoon dry mustard
$1/2$ teaspoon salt
$1/4$ teaspoon coarsely ground pepper
$1/4$ cup vegetable or olive oil
Lemon wedges

1. In a large bowl, beat eggs lightly. Add remaining ingredients, except oil and lemon wedges. Mixture will be thin.

2. In a large skillet, heat oil over medium heat. Drop batter by the spoonful into skillet. Cook until golden; turn over and brown the other side. Transfer to a heated platter and serve immediately. Garnish with lemon wedges.

4 servings

Salmon Stuffed with Lemon Rice

Salmon is caught commercially by purse seiners and gillnetters. Fresh salmon can be purchased from C.O.B. Fish Co. in Anacortes on Fidalgo Island. Prepared ahead of time, this entree can bake while you enjoy a glass of wine with your guests.

1/3 cup butter or margarine
4 green onions, sliced
2 stalks celery, sliced with leaves
1 cup sliced mushrooms
1/4 teaspoon dried thyme
2 tablespoons minced fresh parsley
1 3/4 cups water
1/4 cup fresh lemon juice
1 cup white rice, or part wild rice
1/2 cup sour cream or yogurt
1 (4-8 pound) salmon, dressed, washed and dried
1 lemon, sliced
Parsley sprigs

1. In a large saucepan, melt butter. Sauté onion, celery and mushrooms lightly, about 5 minutes. Season with thyme and parsley.

2. Add water and lemon juice to saucepan and cook rice according to package directions. Remove from heat; add sour cream or yogurt and stir to blend.

3. Preheat oven to 450°. Place salmon on foil and fill salmon cavity with rice mixture. Close opening by sewing or using metal or wooden skewers. Place lemon slices on top of salmon.

4. Wrap salmon in foil and place on baking sheet. Bake for 10 minutes per inch, measured at thickest part and until fish flakes when tested with a fork.

5. Remove dressing to a warmed serving dish. Cut baked salmon into serving pieces and transfer to plates. Garnish with parsley.

1/2 pound salmon per serving

Haro Strait Halibut in Mushroom Sauce

Halibut season is open almost all year, although local fishermen have found March through May to be the most productive months. Enjoy your catch with this piquant sauce.

6 halibut steaks (about 3 pounds)
1/4 cup butter or margarine
1 cup sliced mushrooms
3 green onions, sliced
1 teaspoon Dijon mustard
2 teaspoons fresh lemon juice
1/2 cup sour cream
1/4 cup mayonnaise
Salt and pepper, to taste
Parsley
Paprika

1. Preheat oven to 400°. Arrange steaks in buttered 9x13-inch shallow baking dish. Dot steaks with 2 tablespoons butter and bake for 15 minutes.

2. While halibut is baking, melt remaining butter in saucepan. Sauté mushrooms and onion. Add mustard and lemon juice; mix in sour cream and mayonnaise. Salt and pepper to taste.

3. Pour sauce over steaks. Return to oven and continue cooking for 10 more minutes or until fish flakes with fork. Garnish with parsley and paprika. Serve immediately.   6 servings

Classic Herbed Halibut

Grill or broil this marinated halibut for an elegant meal.

4 tablespoons butter or margarine, melted
1 clove garlic, minced
½ teaspoon salt
⅛ teaspoon freshly ground pepper
2 tablespoons lemon juice
½ cup dry white wine
½ teaspoon dried dill weed or dried tarragon
2 tablespoons fresh chopped parsley
6 halibut steaks (about 3 pounds)
Parsley sprigs
Lemon wedges

1. In a small bowl, make marinade by combining first 8 ingredients. Arrange fish steaks in one layer in a shallow pan. Pour marinade over fish; cover and marinate about 1 hour.

2. Remove fish from marinade and place on greased broiling pan. Broil or grill steaks 2 to 4 inches from heat source for 5 minutes. Turn and baste with remaining marinade, including butter. Continue broiling until fish flakes with fork.

3. Garnish with additional parsley and lemon wedges.   6 servings

Stuffed Halibut Cheeks

Slocum's Restaurant on Fidalgo Island offers a spectacular view overlooking Skyline Marina. Fresh local and exotic seafoods are featured on their menu, along with prime meats.

HOLLANDAISE SAUCE (see page 111)
4 halibut cheeks (about 5 ounces each)
Shortening or vegetable oil
½ pound cooked crab meat and shrimp mixture
¼ cup butter, at room temperature
Flour
2 eggs, lightly beaten
½ cup panko (Japanese style breading)*

1. Prepare Hollandaise Sauce; keep warm until serving time.
2. Cut pocket in each halibut cheek and set aside.
3. Preheat oil in deep-fryer to 300°. In a small bowl, blend crab meat, shrimp and butter. Stuff each halibut pocket with mixture.
4. Dredge each halibut pocket in flour, dip into beaten eggs, then coat with panko breading.
5. Deep-fry halibut pockets 4 minutes or until golden brown. Remove from fryer and drain on paper towels. Serve immediately with Hollandaise Sauce. (To prepare halibut ahead of time: Deep-fry for 2 minutes; remove from fryer and drain on paper towels. Refrigerate until approximately 15 minutes before serving time. Preheat oven to 450°. Place stuffed halibut in oven and heat until internal temperature is 110°, about 10 minutes. Serve immediately.   4 servings

*Available in the Oriental section of most supermarkets.

Halibut Baked in Parchment

Christina's Restaurant in Eastsound on Orcas Island is noted for its fine cuisine and elegant atmosphere. The view of the Sound offers a perfect setting to enjoy a memorable dinner.

6 fresh halibut fillets (about 3 pounds)
Parchment paper
¼ cup melted butter
1 cup sliced mushrooms
½ cup chopped chives
½ cup chopped fresh parsley
½ cup butter, at room temperature
1 clove garlic, minced
1 tablespoon fresh lemon juice
1 tablespoon dry white wine
White pepper, to taste

1. Rinse fillets and remove any bones. Dry between paper towels and set aside.

2. Cut parchment into 6 large heart-shaped pieces, approximately 10½-inches long by 15-inches wide. Brush parchment with melted butter. Fold heart in half lengthwise. Place halibut to one side of center fold. Place equal amounts of mushrooms, chives and parsley on top of each fillet.

3. Preheat oven to 350°. In a small bowl, combine butter, garlic, lemon juice, wine and pepper. Top each fillet with 1½ tablespoons of seasoned butter mixture.

4. Fold parchment in half along previous fold. Start at one end of fold and crimp along open edge to seal; continue around edge until fillet is completely sealed. Place package on a baking sheet. Repeat process with remaining halibut fillets.

5. Bake for 15 minutes or until fish flakes when tested with a fork. Serve in parchment on individual plates.   6 servings

Christina's Lingcod with Ginger Glaze

Owner-chef Christina Gentry offers fresh and seasonal foods of the Pacific Northwest. Guests are delighted to discover this tasteful restaurant in Eastsound on Orcas Island.

6 fresh cod fillets (about 3 pounds)
Glaze
1½ cups mayonnaise (preferably homemade)
1 clove garlic
1 tablespoon white miso*
1 teaspoon rice wine vinegar
2 drops sesame oil
1 teaspoon lime juice
1 walnut-size fresh ginger root, peeled and sliced
1 cup fresh cilantro leaves
Lime wedges

1. Preheat oven to 400°. Rinse fillets and dry between paper towels. Place fillets on a greased baking sheet. Bake 10 minutes or until fish flakes when tested with a fork. Remove from oven and remove bones; set aside.

2. While fish is baking, in a food processor or blender, process glaze ingredients until fine. Add cilantro and process until chopped.

3. Preheat broiler. Place fillets on broiling pan and spread fillets with glaze. Broil until glaze begins to bubble. Remove from oven and serve with a lime wedge.   6 servings

*Available in health food stores or the Oriental section of most supermarkets.

Herb Baked Cod

The cold deep waters of the San Juans are abundant with cod. This is a flavorful variation of pan-fried cod.

4 cod fillets (about 2 pounds)
$\frac{1}{2}$ cup dried bread crumbs
$\frac{1}{4}$ cup grated Parmesan cheese
$\frac{1}{4}$ teaspoon dried dill weed
$\frac{1}{4}$ teaspoon seasoning salt
1 tablespoon minced fresh parsley
$\frac{1}{2}$ cup mayonnaise
1 tablespoon fresh lemon juice

1. Rinse fish and dry between paper towels; set aside.
2. In a pie plate, combine next 5 ingredients.
3. Preheat oven to 425°. Generously coat fish fillets first with mayonnaise and then with crumb mixture. Place fish in buttered 9x13-inch baking dish. Sprinkle with lemon juice.
4. Bake for 10 minutes per inch thickness. Serve with lemon wedges.

4 servings

Crispy Deep Fried Fish Balls

These are so delicate they will melt in your mouth.

2 eggs, separated
1/2 cup milk
1 teaspoon oil
1 cup flour
1/2 teaspoon salt
1 tablespoon lemon juice
2 pounds white fish fillets
TARTAR SAUCE (see page 108)
Lemon wedges

1. In a medium bowl, beat egg yolks until thick. Add remaining ingredients, except fish and egg whites, and mix to blend.

2. In a separate bowl, beat egg whites until stiff. Fold in egg yolk mixture.

3. Cut up fillets into bite-size pieces. Add fish to egg batter. Mixture can be refrigerated for 2 hours at this time. Remove fish balls from batter with a fork; if you use a spoon you will get too much batter.

4. Fry fish balls in hot oil (375°) about 3-4 minutes or until golden. Remove with slotted spoon and drain on paper towels. Keep warm in oven until ready to serve. Serve with tartar sauce and lemon wedges.

4-6 servings

Slocum's Blackened Rockfish

Slocum's Restaurant on Fidalgo Island's Flounder Bay, features only the freshest local seafood. The Cajun spice adds a delightful "zip" to mild rockfish.

4 (8-ounce) rockfish fillets (any white fish will do)
½ cup butter
1 cup clarified butter
2 tablespoons Cajun Red Fish Spice*
Chopped parsley

1. Rinse fish and dry with paper towels; set aside.
2. In a small saucepan, melt ½ cup butter; set aside. In another saucepan, clarify 1 cup butter; keep warm to serve with fish.
3. Heat a cast-iron pan over high heat until a white powder forms on bottom of pan. (Don't worry, you can't get your pan too hot.)
4. While pan is heating, sprinkle both sides of fish fillets with spice. Dip into ½ cup melted butter and place into hot pan. Fillets will flame up briefly and smoke. Cook 1½ minutes per side.
5. Transfer fillets to warm serving plates and serve each with ¼ cup clarified butter for dipping. Garnish fillets with parsley.   4 servings

*Available in most supermarkets.

Strawberry Bay Red Snapper

It is possible to catch the makings for this tasty dish in Strawberry Bay at Cypress Island.

6 snapper fish steaks (about 3 pounds)
2 tablespoons fresh lemon juice
2 tablespoons olive oil
1 medium onion, sliced
2 cloves garlic, minced
1/2 cup chopped celery
1/2 cup chopped green pepper
1/2 cup sliced mushrooms
1/2 cup chopped fresh parsley
1/2 teaspoon dried oregano
1/2 cup dry white wine
2 (16-ounce) cans whole tomatoes, including liquid
1/2 teaspoon salt
1/4 teaspoon pepper
1/4 cup grated Parmesan cheese.

1. Sprinkle snapper with lemon juice and set aside to tenderize. In a skillet, heat oil over medium heat and sauté onion, garlic, celery, green pepper and mushrooms until tender. Add parsley, oregano, wine and canned tomatoes with liquid. Heat to a low simmer and allow to reduce for 10 minutes to thicken sauce.

2. Preheat oven to 350°. Place one-third of vegetable mixture in bottom of a greased 9x13-inch baking dish. Lay fish on top and cover with remaining vegetable mixture. Sprinkle with salt, pepper and Parmesan cheese. Bake for 30 to 40 minutes or until fish flakes when tested with a fork. Serve over rice.

6 servings

Stuffed Fillet of Sole

The delicate taste of sole is enhanced by the flavored rice stuffing and creamy sauce.

1 (10-ounce) package frozen chopped spinach or ¾ pound fresh spinach, chopped
3 cups cooked rice
3 hard-cooked eggs, chopped
¼ cup chopped fresh parsley
4 green onions, chopped
2 tablespoons mayonnaise
6 medium-size sole fillets
Dill Sauce
5 tablespoons butter or margarine
¼ cup flour
½ teaspoon salt
2 cups milk
¼ cup dry white wine
½ teaspoon dried dill weed

1. Thaw frozen spinach or steam fresh spinach about 5 minutes; squeeze out excess moisture.

2. In a large bowl, combine spinach and rice. Place 2 cups rice mixture in bottom of buttered 9x13-inch baking dish.

3. To remaining rice mixture add eggs, parsley, onion, and mayonnaise. Divide mixture among fillets and roll fillets over to close. Set fillet rolls, seam side down, on rice and spinach mixture in baking dish. Preheat oven to 350°.

4. To prepare Dill Sauce, melt butter in a small saucepan. Blend in flour and salt. Gradually whisk in milk, stirring constantly until mixture thickens; do not boil. Remove from heat.

5. Stir wine and dill weed into sauce; pour over fish fillets and cover with foil. Dish may be refrigerated at this point.

6. Bake, covered, for 35 minutes (45 minutes, if refrigerated) or until fish flakes when tested with a fork. Serve immediately.

6 servings

Crab Burgers

It is fun to find a Dungeness crab while walking through eel grass on the tide flats. These puffy crab burgers can easily be made from one crab.

GARLIC MAYONNAISE (see below)
1½ - 2 cups cooked crab meat
2 teaspoons Worcestershire sauce
3 chopped green onions, without tops
1½ tablespoons chopped parsley
Dash Tabasco sauce
½ teaspoon salt
¼ teaspoon pepper
3 eggs, separated
2 tablespoons butter
2 tablespoons vegetable oil
6 whole wheat hamburger buns
6 lettuce leaves
1 tomato, sliced

1. Prepare Garlic Mayonnaise; cover and chill until needed.

2. In a medium bowl, combine crab meat with Worcestershire sauce, onion, parsley, Tabasco sauce, salt and pepper.

3. Separate eggs, beat yolks and add to crab mixture. In a clean bowl, beat egg whites until stiff and fold into crab mixture.

4. In a large frying pan, heat butter and oil over medium heat. Cook crab burgers until golden brown, turning once.

5. Butter the bun halves and broil until lightly toasted. Spread with Garlic Mayonnaise. Place crab burgers, lettuce and tomato on buns. 6 servings

GARLIC MAYONNAISE

⅓ cup mayonnaise
1 clove garlic, minced

In a small bowl, combine mayonnaise and garlic.

Crab Fettucine

Dungeness crab can be caught with crab rings throughout the year. The season for crab pots is August through May. This dish is a visual, as well as a gastronomic, delight.

3 tablespoons butter
3 tablespoons olive oil
2 cloves garlic, minced
2 tomatoes, peeled, seeded and chopped
½ cup dry white wine
¾-1 cup heavy cream (whipping)
1 pound fettucine
2 tablespoons PESTO SAUCE (optional)
2 tablespoons olive oil
1½ teaspoons dry or ¼ cup finely chopped fresh basil
2 cups cooked crab meat
¼ cup chopped fresh parsley
¼ cup fresh Parmesan cheese, grated
Salt and coarsely ground pepper, to taste
Parsley
Parmesan cheese

1. In a large skillet, over medium heat, melt butter and olive oil. Add the garlic and sauté 2 minutes; add tomatoes and simmer until softened. Add wine and heat; stir in cream. Simmer to reduce, 10 minutes. Do not boil.

2. In a large pot, cook pasta al dente, according to package directions. Drain, return to cooking pot and stir in Pesto and oil to coat pasta. Cover to keep warm.

3. Add basil, crab and parsley to sauce. Simmer 5 minutes to heat through and bend flavors. Gently add Parmesan. Salt and pepper to taste.

4. Turn pasta onto warmed serving platter; pour sauce over pasta. Garnish with additional parsley and Parmesan.   4 servings.

Kim's Crab Quiche

The ingredients in the rich custard can be varied.

1 10-inch unbaked pie shell
1 tablespoon butter
$^1/_3$ cup chopped onion
$^1/_3$ cup diced green bell pepper
$^1/_3$ cup diced red pepper
$^1/_2$ cup sliced mushrooms
$^1/_2$ cup cooked crab meat
1 (7-ounce) can artichoke hearts, drained and sliced
$^1/_3$ cup sliced ripe olives
4 eggs
2 cups light cream
$^1/_4$ teaspoon dry mustard
Dash cayenne pepper
$^1/_4$ teaspoon salt
$^1/_8$ teaspoon freshly ground pepper
$^3/_4$ cup grated Swiss cheese

1. Preheat oven to 375°. Bake pie shell for 7 minutes. Remove from oven and cool on a wire rack.

2. In a medium skillet, melt butter and sauté onion, peppers and mushrooms until onion is soft. Remove from heat, add crab meat, artichoke hearts and olives; set aside.

3. In a large bowl, beat eggs lightly. Add cream, mustard, cayenne, salt and pepper; set aside.

4. Sprinkle the cheese on the bottom of the pie shell. Add reserved onion mixture; pour in egg mixture. Bake for 45 minutes or until knife inserted in center comes out clean. Cool 5 minutes before serving.

6-8 servings

Deviled Crab

Laura Burton on Fidalgo Island serves this flavorful entree in gratin dishes for an elegant company dinner.

4 tablespoons butter or margarine
2 tablespoons chopped onion
2 tablespoons chopped green pepper
3 cups crab meat, shrimp, or combination
2 tablespoons flour
1 teaspoon Worcestershire sauce
1 teaspoon cayenne pepper
1 teaspoon dry mustard
1 teaspoon salt
Dash pepper
1 cup heavy cream
⅓ cup dry bread crumbs
2 tablespoons butter, melted
4 teaspoons grated Parmesan cheese (optional)

1. In a medium saucepan, melt butter over medium heat. Sauté onion and green pepper until soft. Add seafood and sprinkle with flour; stir in seasonings. Preheat oven to 400°.

2. Remove pan from heat and stir in cream. Spoon crab mixture into individual baking dishes or shells. Top each with a heaping tablespoon of bread crumbs and drizzle with 1 teaspoon melted butter. Sprinkle each with 1 teaspoon Parmesan, if desired. Bake for 15 minutes.

4 servings

Grilled Crab and Cheese Sandwiches

The waters off Saddlebag Island in Padilla Bay abound with Dungeness crab. These delectable sandwiches will satisfy any hungry crab eater.

$1/2$ cup mayonnaise
$1/4$ cup chili sauce
$1/4$ cup chopped celery
4 green onions, chopped
2 cups Dungeness crab
3 cups grated cheddar cheese
12 slices of your favorite bread
Butter

1. In a medium mixing bowl, stir together mayonnaise, chili sauce, celery, and green onions. Add crab and grated cheese, blending well.

2. Butter one side of 6 bread slices and place buttered side down in a large frying pan; spread filling on bread slices. Butter remaining 6 slices of bread and place on top of filling.

3. Grill sandwiches over medium heat, as you would a traditional grilled cheese sandwich until cheese melts and bread is toasted. Cover, if necessary, to heat insides. Slice and serve immediately.   6-8 servings

Baked Oysters on the Half Shell

Downriggers Restaurant in Friday Harbor on San Juan Island serves Westcott Bay oysters in a savory Herb Butter. While enjoying the fine food, guests are also treated to a spectacular view of the harbor.

24 small Westcott Bay oysters, on the half shell
Rock salt
HERB BUTTER (see below)
Brandy
1/4 cup freshly grated Parmesan cheese

1. Line bottom of a broiling pan with rock salt. Arrange oysters on the half shell over rock salt.
2. Prepare Herb Butter.
3. Place one heaping teaspoon of the Herb Butter on each oyster. Add a dash of brandy and top with 1/2 teaspoon Parmesan cheese.
4. Bake at 375° for 10 minutes or until golden brown.   4 servings

HERB BUTTER

1/2 cup butter, at room temperature
1/4 teaspoon thyme
1/2 teaspoon minced fresh parsley
1/2 teaspoon dried basil
1/2 teaspoon dried rosemary

In a small bowl, whip together until double in volume.   1/2 cup

Old-Fashioned Scalloped Oysters

Oysters, once abundant on rocky shores in the San Juans are rarely found today. Commercially grown oysters are harvested daily and available at Similk Bay on Fidalgo Island. This is a traditional oyster dish that is always a favorite.

½ cup melted butter
2 cups soda cracker crumbs
1 pint shucked oysters (drained reserving ¼ cup liquid)
Salt and freshly ground pepper
2 tablespoons chopped parsley
¾ cup milk or cream
½ teaspoon Worcestershire sauce
¼ teaspoon cayenne

1. In a medium bowl, combine melted butter and cracker crumbs. Place one-half of the crumb mixture in the bottom of a buttered pie plate or 1 quart casserole.

2. Layer oysters onto cracker crumbs. Large oysters can be cut in half. Season lightly with salt and pepper and sprinkle with 1 tablespoon parsley.

3. Preheat oven to 350°. In a small bowl, combine oyster liquid and milk, Worcestershire sauce and cayenne. Pour over oysters.

4. Top with remaining crumb mixture and 1 tablespoon parsley. Bake uncovered for 30 minutes or until golden brown.   4-6 servings

Oysters Rockefeller

A classic dish for a memorable luncheon or a midnight supper.

24 oysters, shucked (keep the cupped bottom shell)
1/2 pound spinach, washed and chopped or 1 (10-ounce) package frozen chopped
   spinach (defrosted with moisture removed)
1/2 cup butter
6-8 green onions, minced
1/2 cup minced fresh parsley
1 clove garlic, minced
1 tablespoon Worcestershire sauce
2 dashes Tabasco sauce
2 teaspoons lemon juice
Salt and pepper, to taste
1/2 cup fine bread crumbs
1/4 cup grated Parmesan cheese
Rock salt
Lemon wedges

1. Melt butter in frying pan, without browning. Sauté onion, parsley and garlic lightly. Add spinach; cover and cook until wilted and heated through.

2. Stir in Worcestershire sauce, Tabasco sauce and lemon juice. Salt and pepper to taste; mix well. This can be made ahead and refrigerated.

3. Preheat oven to 450°. Fill broiler pan with rock salt. Place oyster shell halves, cup side down, on salt. Spoon spinach mixture over oysters. Sprinkle with bread crumbs and Parmesan.

4. Bake until oyster edges curl, about 5 minutes. Serve with lemon wedges.

4 servings

Steamed Oysters à la Westcott

We visited with Bill and Doe Webb at their aquaculture farm on San Juan Island. At Westcott Bay Sea Farms they have developed a method of growing selected oysters suspended in the water in Japanesse lantern nets. Westcott Farms provides gourmet oysters to restaurants from New York City to Fairbanks, Alaska.

JOY'S SAUCE (recipe follows)
4 dozen small Westcott Bay Oysters
Water
Parsley sprigs
Lemon wedges

1. Prepare Joy's Sauce and set aside.
2. In a large kettle, place oysters in 1-inch of water. Cover and steam until shells are barely open, about 5 minutes.
3. Remove top shell from each oyster and discard. Arrange oysters on 4 serving plates. Spoon Pesto Sauce over each oyster. Garnish with parsley and lemon wedges. Serve with French bread and pasta.   4 servings

JOY'S SAUCE

½ cup butter
2 cloves garlic, minced
2 tablespoons fresh lemon juice
1 teaspoon dried basil or 1 tablespoon fresh chopped basil
½ teaspoon coarsely ground black pepper

1. In a large saucepan, melt butter over medium heat and sauté garlic.
2. Add lemon juice, basil and pepper. Heat through and keep sauce warm to serve over oysters.

Oysters in the Shell with Shallot Sauce

For a memorable beach party, bring this savory shallot sauce and a bag of oysters.

½ cup butter
2 medium shallots or green onions, minced
¼ teaspoon dried tarragon
½ teaspoon coarsely ground pepper
2 tablespoons freshly chopped parsley
¼ cup lemon juice
24 oysters, in the shell

1. In a small saucepan, melt butter and sauté shallots or onions, about 2 minutes. Remove from heat; add tarragon, pepper, parsley and lemon juice. Stir to blend. Sauce can be made ahead and stored up to 1 week in the refrigerator, if desired.

2. Rinse oyster shells. With cupped side down, place on pre-heated grill, about 4 inches from hot coals. Grill about 10 minutes or until shells begin to open. Remove top shell and pour 1 tablespoon heated shallot sauce over each oyster. Grill 4 minutes longer, until sauce bubbles. Do not overcook.   4 servings

Clams on the Half Shell

This old family favorite is requested whenever there is a clam tide. The toasted bread crumbs and olive oil impart a nuttiness to the clams. Clean the clams by soaking overnight in a large bucket of salt water.

24 large butter clams, shells cleaned
3 eggs, slightly beaten
1 cup dried seasoned bread crumbs
¼ - ½ cup olive oil
Lemon wedges

1. To open clams, remove them carefully from the water, one at a time, to prevent the resting clams from closing tightly.

2. With a thin blade, cut into meat of clam near thick end of shell. Run blade through entire clam, cutting the muscle. Break shell in half. Remove stomach from both halves. Rinse, turn over and drain on paper towels. Continue until all clams are cleaned.

3. In a large frying pan, heat oil over medium-high heat. Dip clams in shell, meat side down, into egg and then into crumbs. Fry them, meat side down, until they are crispy brown, about 4 minutes. Add more oil as needed. Remove to platter lined with paper towels; keep warm in oven. Serve in the shells with lemon wedges.

4 servings

Clam Fritters

Joanne Funk's savory fritters are ample reward for the effort of digging butter clams at low tide.

6 eggs, beaten
2 cups coarsely ground clams
1/4 teaspoon seafood seasoning or seasoned salt
1 tablespoon minced fresh parsley
1 small onion, finely chopped
1/4 cup chopped green pepper
1 teaspoon Worcestershire sauce
1 1/2 cups saltine cracker crumbs
1/4 cup butter
Lemon wedges

1. In a medium bowl, combine all ingredients, except cracker crumbs and butter. Add crumbs to mixture 1/2 cup at a time until mixture makes a stiff batter.

2. In a large skillet, melt butter over medium high heat. Spoon batter into skillet. Cook until golden, turn over and brown the other side. Transfer to a heated platter and serve immediately. Garnish with lemon wedges.

4-6 servings

Clamguine

This recipe is a favorite at North Beach on Guemes Island. With crusty French bread and a green salad, it is a complete meal.

1 pound linguine
2 tablespoons olive oil
2 tablespoons PESTO SAUCE (optional)
4 tablespoons olive oil
4 cloves garlic, minced
2 cups minced clams, fresh or canned, including nectar
½ cup dry white wine (optional)
1 cup chopped fresh parsley
1 teaspoon dried oregano
Salt and finely ground pepper, to taste
⅓ cup grated fresh Parmesan cheese

1. In a large pot, cook linguine al dente, according to package directions. Drain and return to pot. Stir in 2 tablespoons oil and Pesto Sauce to coat pasta. Cover to keep warm.

2. While pasta is cooking, heat 4 tablespoons oil in heavy skillet over medium heat. Add garlic and sauté until golden, about 1 minute; do not burn. Add clams, including nectar, wine, parsley and oregano. Simmer until clams are cooked, 10 minutes for fresh clams, 5 minutes for canned clams. Do not overcook. Salt and pepper to taste.

3. Place linguine on a heated platter. Spoon clam sauce over linguine. Sprinkle with Parmesan. Serve with additional Parmesan.   6 servings

Milo's Mighty Mussels

Chef-proprietor Michael Hood of Barkley's Restaurant in La Conner serves Lopez Mussel Company or Penn Cove mussels in a delicious cream sauce. Serve with crusty French bread to sop up the delicious sauce.

2 pounds mussels, debearded and scrubbed
1 cup dry vermouth
4 cups whipping cream
2 teaspoons dried oregano
2 lemons
Minced parsley

1. In a large skillet, place mussels and vermouth. Steam over high heat until mussels open and are firm, about 5 minutes. With a slotted spoon, remove mussels; set aside and cover to keep warm. Pour off mussel liquid and reserve.

2. Into the same skillet, pour cream, 2 cups reserved mussel liquid and oregano. Save any additional mussel liquid for another use. Simmer sauce until it reduces and thickens.

3. Put mussels into four serving bowls and pour sauce over mussels. Squeeze ½ lemon over each bowl of mussels and sprinkle with parsley. Serve immediately.   4 servings

Jeanna's Mussels in White Wine and Herbs

Enjoy fresh local mussels steamed with herbs and vegetables at Jeanna's Seafood Gallery on Lopez Island. Save room for one of their delectable desserts.

  3 pounds mussels
  1 cup water
  1 cup dry white wine
  1 teaspoon dried thyme
  1 teaspoon dried tarragon
  1 teaspoon dried basil
  $^1/_2$ cup chopped celery
  $^1/_2$ cup diced onion
  Salt and freshly ground pepper, to taste
  Lemon wedges
  Parsley sprigs
  Clarified butter

1. Scrub mussels and debeard; set aside in colander.
2. In a large pot, bring water and wine to a boil; add mussels and remaining ingredients. Steam about 7 minutes or until mussels are open.
3. Place mussels in serving bowls; pour liquid over mussels. Garnish with lemon and parsley; serve with clarified butter.   4-6 servings

Sautéed Prawns or Scallops

Thibert's Crab Market on Fidalgo Island is popular for its wide variety of fresh local and exotic seafoods. Here is an elegant entree to enjoy with our Spinach Caesar Salad.

2 pounds medium-size prawns or scallops, shelled and deveined
½ cup butter
2-3 cloves garlic, minced
3 tablespoons chopped green onions
2 cups sliced mushrooms (optional)
½ teaspoon dried tarragon
½ cup dry white wine
1½ tablespoons fresh lemon juice
2 tablespoons chopped fresh parsley
Salt and pepper, to taste
Lemon wedges

1. Wash prawns or scallops and dry with paper towel; set aside.

2. In large frying pan, melt butter and add garlic, onion, mushrooms and tarragon. Sauté until vegetables are softened. Add prawns or scallops; sauté about 5 minutes.

3. Pour in wine and lemon juice. Gently stir in parsley. Simmer to blend flavors, about 3 minutes. Salt and pepper to taste. Serve with lemon wedges.

4 servings

Seafood Crepes

Jeanna's Seafood Gallery on Lopez Island features fresh local and exotic seafood in their fish market and restaurant.

Crepes
3 eggs
1 cup milk
⅔ cup unsifted all-purpose flour
¼ cup butter
Filling
1½ pounds mixed seafood (bay scallops, shrimp, white fish, salmon) cut into
    ¼-inch cubes
1 cup clarified butter
½ cup dry white wine
2 tablespoons dried tarragon
1 teaspoon dried basil
3 cloves garlic, minced
Salt and pepper, to taste
2 cups heavy cream

1. To prepare crepes: In a blender, combine eggs and milk; add unsifted flour. Cover and process until smooth.

2. In a 6 to 8-inch crepe pan, melt 1 teaspoon butter over medium heat. Coat pan surface with butter. Pour 2 tablespoons batter into pan and tilt to cover pan bottom with a thin layer of batter. Cook crepes until edges are browned and surface appears dry; turn and cook other side a few seconds. Remove from pan and place on a plate; cover with foil to keep warm.

3. To prepare filling: In a medium skillet, sauté seafood in clarified butter over medium heat. Add wine, herbs and seasonings; continue cooking until wine reduces and seafood is tender. Remove ½ cup of seafood mixture with a slotted spoon and place on crepe. Roll crepe and place on a platter seam side down; keep warm in oven. Repeat steps for remaining crepes.

4. To wine mixture in skillet, add cream and reduce until sauce is thick and small bubbles appear. Pour sauce over warm crepes and serve immediately. This rich entree is best accompanied by mild side dishes, such as rice and steamed vegetables.   4 servings

Curried Shrimp or Chicken

This lively curry sauce enhances a quick entree that is always enjoyed.

1/4 cup butter
3 tablespoons chopped onion
1/4 cup finely chopped tart apple
3 tablespoons flour
1-2 teaspoons curry powder
1/4 teaspoon ground ginger
Dash cayenne pepper
1 cup CHICKEN STOCK
1 cup light cream
2 cups diced cooked chicken or cooked shrimp
Salt and pepper, to taste
Steamed rice
Raisins, peanuts, chutney, coconut (condiments)

1. In a medium saucepan, melt butter, sauté onion and apple over low heat until onion is soft. Blend in flour, curry powder, ginger and cayenne pepper. Cook and stir for about 2 minutes.

2. Add Chicken Stock and cream, stirring to blend. Cook for approximately 10 minutes, stirring occasionally. When sauce begins to thicken, add chicken or shrimp. Salt and pepper to taste. Serve over steamed rice. Place condiments in a small bowl.   4 servings

Seafood Newburg à la Roche Harbor

Roche Harbor on San Juan Island was developed in 1886 as a company town for a limestone quarry. The quiet elegance of the historic Hotel de Haro is complimented by the newly remodeled restaurant. The rich combination of Seafood Newburg is often requested by returning guests.

6 ounces small bay scallops
5 tablespoons butter
1 tablespoon finely chopped shallots
1/2 teaspoon paprika
5 tablespoons flour
2 cups milk
1 cup whipping cream
4 tablespoons butter
8 ounces raw lobster meat, cut into 3/4-inch chunks
6 ounces raw shrimp, peeled and deveined, tails left on
8 ounces fresh mushrooms, sliced
6 ounces Dungeness crab meat, cooked
2 tablespoons dry sherry
Dash cayenne pepper
Salt, to taste

1. In a small saucepan, poach scallops in 1-inch boiling water for 1 to 2 minutes. Drain and set aside.

2. In a medium saucepan, melt butter, sauté shallots until soft. Blend in paprika and flour, cook 3 to 5 minutes; do not burn. Gradually whisk in milk and cream. Stir constantly until sauce thickens; set aside.

3. In a large skillet, melt butter, sauté lobster, shrimp and mushrooms until almost cooked, about 10 minutes. Add crab meat and reserved scallops.

4. Sprinkle sherry over seafood, gently stir in reserved cream sauce. Bring mixture to a boil; remove from heat immediately. Season with cayenne and salt to taste. Serve immediately over rice or in a pastry shell.

6 servings

Paella San Juan

Early Pacific Northwest explorers might have enjoyed their own version of this Spanish dish while sailing through the San Juan waters.

2 tablespoons butter or margarine
1 whole chicken breast, skinned, boned and cut into 4 pieces
1/4 cup olive oil
2 cloves garlic, minced
1 onion, chopped
1 tomato, peeled, seeded and chopped
1 green pepper, seeded and chopped
1 chorizo (hot Spanish sausage), sliced
2 cups long grain rice
1/2 cup dry white wine
4 cups CHICKEN STOCK
1 teaspoon saffron
1 teaspoon dried oregano
1 1/2 teaspoons salt
1/2 teaspoon coarsely ground pepper
8 large shrimp, washed and deveined
20 steamer clams, washed
24 mussels, washed and debearded
1 cup fresh or frozen peas
1 (4-ounce) can pimiento, sliced
1/2 cup sliced black olives
1/4 cup chopped fresh parsley
Lemon wedges

1. In a large oven-proof skillet or paellero, melt butter over medium heat. Sauté chicken on both sides until golden brown. Remove chicken with a slotted spoon and set aside.

2. In the same skillet, heat olive oil and sauté garlic, onion, tomato, green pepper and chorizo until vegetables are tender. Remove with a slotted spoon and set aside.

3. Add rice to skillet and lightly brown. Return vegetables and chorizo to skillet. Add wine, Chicken Stock, saffron, oregano, salt and pepper. Simmer for 1 minute on medium-high. Stir and reduce heat to medium. Cover and cook about 12 minutes or until rice has soaked up about 80% of the liquid. Add reserved chicken to rice and turn rice top to bottom.

4. Preheat oven to 375°. Lay shrimp, clams and mussels on rice. Sprinkle with peas, pimiento, olives and parsley. Cover and bake for 15 minutes or until shellfish has opened. Remove paella from the oven and serve with lemon wedges. 4 servings.

Seviche

This Mexican dish, popular in the Pacific Northwest, is refreshing on warm summer evenings. The lime juice "cooks" the scallops or fish.

1 pound bay scallops or boneless white fish fillets
1 cup fresh lime juice
2 ripe tomatoes, peeled, seeded and cut into ¼-inch cubes
1 clove garlic, minced
2 tablespoons finely chopped cilantro (Mexican parsley)
¼ teaspoon crushed hot red pepper flakes
4 green onions, chopped fine
1 firm avocado, diced
Salt and freshly ground pepper, to taste
Lettuce greens, washed and dried

1. If using the fish, cut into small cubes. Place fish or scallops in a bowl and toss with fresh juice.
2. Add tomatoes, garlic, parsley and red pepper; stir to blend. Cover and chill overnight.
3. Before serving, add chopped green onions and avocado. Salt and pepper to taste. Serve on a bed of crisp lettuce on chilled salad plates.

6 servings

Calamari

Calamari can be served as an appetizer or as a main dish prepared at the table with guests.

AIOLI SAUCE (see page 108)
2 pounds squid
1½ cups flour
1 teaspoon black pepper
½ teaspoon garlic salt
½ teaspoon dry mustard
1½ teaspoon paprika
Peanut oil

1. Prepare Aioli Sauce, cover and refrigerate.
2. To clean squid, pull body from hood, remove pen (transparent back-bone), viscera and discard. Cut body between eyes and tentacles, and dis-card body. Cut hoods into ¼ to ½-inch wide rings; drain rings and tenta-cles on paper towel.
3. In a medium bowl, combine remaining ingredients except oil.
4. In a wok or deep pan, heat 2-inches of oil to 350°. Do not allow oil to get to the smoking point. Dust rings and tentacles with flour mixture and deep-fry about 1 minute. (Do not put in too many pieces at once or it will lower the temperature of the oil. Be sure to separate pieces as they cook.) Remove calamari from oil with a slotted spoon and drain on paper towels. Repeat with remaining calamari.
5. Serve warm with Aioli Sauce as a dip.   4-6 servings

Beach Cooked Crab

The best way to cook fresh crab is over an open fire on the beach. Use sea water for just the right flavor.

6 quarts sea water
3 Dungeness crab
Lemon wedges
CRAB LOUIS SAUCE (see page 109)

1. In a large kettle, bring water to a boil. Drop crab, upside down into water. Return water to a boil and cook covered, for 15 minutes.

2. Remove crab from water with tongs and immerse in cold water. When cool, clean crab by pulling off top shell; remove gills and yellow fat. Rinse well with cold water.

3. Crack crab bodies in half and place in a bowl with cracked ice. Serve with lemon wedges and Crab Louis Sauce.   4-6 servings

Abalone

Abalone is a highly prized shellfish because of its sweet flavor and the difficulty in obtaining it. It is possible to find abalone in the waters off many of the rockier San Juan Islands at low tide.

    4-6 abalone steaks (1½ pounds)
    ½ cup flour
    ¼ teaspoon salt
    ⅛ teaspoon pepper
    ¼ teaspoon paprika
    4 tablespoons butter or margarine
    Lemon wedges

1. If you are able to get abalone in the shell, with a sharp knife, cut between the shell and meat, removing the meat. Trim off any dark areas and discard. To tenderize the abalone, place meat between plastic wrap and pound with a mallet until meat is limp. Cut abalone into desired serving pieces and set aside.

2. In a small bowl, combine flour, salt, pepper and paprika; set aside.

3. In a large skillet, heat butter over medium-high heat. Lightly dust abalone steaks with flour mixture. Quickly sauté steaks in butter approximately one minute on each side. Do not overcook as abalone will become tough.

4. Transfer steaks to warm serving plates and garnish with lemon wedges.   4 servings

Aioli Sauce

This versatile garlic-mayonnaise sauce is perfect with fresh fish, fried calamari or vegetables.

4-6 cloves garlic
3 egg yolks
1/3 cup fresh lemon juice
1/2 teaspoon salt
1/4 teaspoon coarsely ground pepper
1/2 cup olive oil
1/2 cup salad oil

1. Before preparing Aioli Sauce, have all ingredients measured and ready. In a food processor or blender, purée garlic. Add egg yolks, lemon juice, salt and pepper and blend.

2. While machine is running, slowly pour oils into mixture; blend until mixture is thick. Cover and chill until ready to use. Aioli Sauce will keep for 4 days.   1 1/2 cups

Tartar Sauce

Our favorite sauce to serve with fish or oysters. The capers add a unique flavor.

1 cup mayonnaise
1/2 cup sour cream
1/4 cup finely chopped dill pickle
3 green onions, thinly sliced
1 teaspoon capers
2 tablespoons minced fresh parsley
1 teaspoon Worcestershire sauce
1 teaspoon dried dill weed
Salt and freshly ground pepper, to taste

In a bowl, combine all ingredients and blend until smooth. Cover and chill.   2 cups

Barbecue Sauce for Fish

This is a delicious sauce for salmon or white fish that is cooked in an oven or on a barbecue.

1/2 cup butter
1 clove garlic, minced
1/4 cup catsup
2 tablespoons soy sauce
1 tablespoon prepared mustard
1 teaspoon Worcestershire sauce
1 tablespoon fresh lemon juice
1/8 teaspoon pepper

1. In a saucepan over medium heat, melt butter and sauté garlic. Be careful not to burn. Add all remaining ingredients and simmer 15 minutes.

2. As fish is cooking, baste with sauce. Serve additional sauce at the table, if desired. 1 cup

Crab Louis Sauce

For a traditional Crab Louis Salad serve this sauce with hard-boiled eggs, tomatoes, black olives, crab and lettuce. Served alone, this sauce is excellent for dipping fresh crab.

1 cup mayonnaise
1/4 cup chili sauce
1 teaspoon Worcestershire sauce
2 tablespoons lemon juice

In a small bowl, combine all ingredients and blend until smooth. Cover and chill. 1 1/4 cups

Dill Sauce

Serve with grilled, poached or baked fish.

>   ¾ cup mayonnaise
>   ¼ cup sour cream
>   2 tablespoons fresh lemon juice
>   1½ teaspoon dried dill weed or 1 tablespoon fresh dill sprigs
>   ½ teaspoon salt
>   ¼ teaspoon white pepper
>   1 teaspoon Dijon mustard (optional)

In a bowl, combine all ingredients and blend until smooth. Cover and chill. 1 cup

Cucumber Sauce

A refreshing sauce to serve with grilled, poached or baked fish.

>   1 medium cucumber, peeled, seeded and finely chopped
>   ¼ teaspoon salt
>   1 tablespoon chopped green onions
>   ¼ teaspoon dried dill weed
>   1 tablespoon lemon juice
>   1 cup sour cream or unflavored yogurt
>   ¼ cup mayonnaise

1. In a medium bowl, place chopped cucumbers and sprinkle with salt. Let rest about 5 minutes; drain. Press out excess moisture with paper towels. Return cucumbers to bowl.
2. Mix remaining ingredients with cucumbers. Chill at least 1 hour.

2 cups

Herb Marinade

This is an excellent marinade for grilled, broiled or baked fish.

1/4 cup finely chopped green onions
1/2 teaspoon dried basil
1/4 teaspoon dried oregano
3 tablespoons soy sauce
1/4 cup lemon juice
1/2 cup vegetable or olive oil
1/8 teaspoon pepper

In a small bowl, mix all ingredients. Marinate fish for at least one hour. Remove fish from marinade to cook. Use marinade as a baste, if desired.

1 cup

Hollandaise Sauce

A classic sauce served over fish or cooked vegetables.

1/2 cup butter
3 egg yolks, at room temperature
1 tablespoon fresh lemon juice
Dash cayenne pepper
1/4 teaspoon salt

1. In a small saucepan, melt butter until it bubbles; do not brown.
2. In a blender, beat egg yolks and lemon juice; turn blender on low speed and gradually add hot butter. Season with cayenne and salt; blend until sauce is thickened and smooth. Keep sauce warm in a double-boiler over hot, not boiling water.

3/4 cup

Seasoned Butters

To add an elegant touch to a meal use one of our seasoned butters as a baste or serve with broiled fish or meats.

TARRAGON BUTTER

    1 teaspoon tarragon
    1½ teaspoons tarragon vinegar
    ½ cup butter, at room temperature

In a small bowl or mixer, combine all ingredients. Form into a 1-inch thick sausage shape on plastic wrap. Wrap tightly and chill for at least 1 hour.

RED PEPPER BUTTER

    2 teaspoons dried red peppers
    1 clove garlic, minced
    1½ teaspoons fresh lemon juice
    ½ cup butter, at room temperature

In a small bowl or mixer, combine all ingredients. Form into a 1-inch thick sausage shape on plastic wrap. Wrap tightly and chill for at least 1 hour.

DILL BUTTER

    ⅓ cup chopped fresh parsley
    2 green onions, chopped
    ½ cup fresh dill sprigs or 2½ tablespoons dried dill
    2 tablespoons fresh chopped tarragon or 2 teaspoons dried
    2 tablespoons fresh lemon juice
    ¾ cup butter, at room temperature

In a small bowl or mixer, combine all ingredients. Form into a 1-inch thick sausage shape on plastic wrap. Wrap tightly and chill for at least 1 hour.

Entrees

Peter Capen

Lime Kiln Lighthouse

Grilled Sante Fe Beef Strips

Chef-proprietor Jeanette Jernigan of Winston's Restaurant in Friday Harbor is respected for her innovative cuisine. Islanders return to partake of an old favorite from the menu or a new dish that she has created. We enjoyed this entree and were pleased she chose to share it with us.

Marinade
1 cup olive oil
1/3 cup lime juice
1/2 cup beer
1 tablespoon minced garlic
1 tablespoon chili powder
1/2 teaspoon red chili flakes
Salsa
1/4 cup olive oil
1/2 large onion, diced
1 stalk celery, diced
1 green pepper, diced
1 cup chopped cilantro
1/3 cup lime juice
4 tomatoes, chopped
1 tablespoon chili powder
1 teaspoon salt
1 tablespoon minced garlic
1 teaspoon dried oregano
1 tablespoon red pepper flakes
1-4 tablespoons chopped fresh Anaheim chilies, depending on desired hotness

1 (2-pound) New York steak strip
1 red bell pepper, cut into 3/8-inch slices
1 green pepper, cut into 3/8-inch slices

1. In a medium saucepan, mix together all marinade ingredients; simmer for 5 minutes. Remove from heat to cool slightly; set aside.

2. In another medium saucepan, heat olive oil over medium heat; sauté onion, celery, and green pepper until soft. Add remaining 9 salsa ingredients and bring to a boil. Reduce heat and simmer 5 minutes; set aside.

3. Cut steak into 1/2-inch thick strips. Place in marinade and toss to coat; allow to marinate for 15 minutes. Grill strips over very hot charbroiler or coals for 1 to 2 minutes on each side. Brush with marinade during cooking. Grill strips of red and green peppers at the same time.

4. Place steak strips on warm plates. Spoon salsa over steak and garnish with grilled peppers.   6 servings

Beef and Broccoli Stir-Fry

This is an appealing quick meal for family or guests. Try other vegetables, such as cauliflower, celery, green pepper or snow peas.

    4 tablespoons vegetable oil
    1 pound sirloin steak, sliced into 1/4-inch strips
    1/2 cup chopped onion
    1 clove garlic, minced
    1/2 pound broccoli, cut into small flowerets
    1 cup sliced mushrooms
    1 small zucchini, sliced
    1/2 cup BEEF STOCK
    1 cup water
    2 tablespoons soy sauce
    1 tablespoon cornstarch

1. In a frying pan or wok, heat 2 tablespoons oil over high heat. Stir-fry meat until lightly browned, about 3 minutes. Remove the meat from pan and set aside.

2. Add remaining 2 tablespoons of oil to pan; sauté onion, garlic, broccoli, mushrooms and zucchini until tender-crisp, about 5 minutes. Reduce heat to medium.

3. In a small bowl, combine Beef Stock, water, soy sauce and cornstarch; be sure there are no lumps. Pour liquid into vegetables and add reserved meat. Cook until sauce thickens; stir occasionally to blend. Serve over rice.

4 servings

Beef Stew with Parsleyed Dumplings

A rich sauce and a hint of curry make this dish a welcome change from traditional stew.

1/4 cup vegetable oil
1 cup chopped onion
1 1/2 cups sliced mushrooms
2 pounds lean beef stew meat
1/2 cup flour
1 1/2 cups beef broth
1 1/2 cups water
1 teaspoon curry powder
Salt and coarsely ground pepper, to taste
DUMPLINGS (recipe follows)
2 cups frozen peas

1. In a Dutch oven, heat oil over medium heat. Sauté onion and mushrooms until onion is soft; remove from pan and set aside.

2. Coat beef with flour; reserve excess flour. In Dutch oven, brown meat on all sides, about 6 or 7 pieces at a time. Add more oil, if necessary.

3. Remove all meat from pan. Pour reserved flour (approximately 3 tablespoons) into oil remaining in pan; stir and cook 2 minutes. Add beef broth and water; simmer until slightly thickened. Add cooked onion, mushrooms, meat and curry. Salt and pepper to taste.

4. Heat to boiling, then reduce heat, cover and simmer for 1 1/2 hours. While stew simmers, prepare Dumplings.

5. Add additional water to Dutch oven so that liquid totals about 3 cups; add peas to stew. Drop spoonfuls of dough onto simmering stew. Cook uncovered for 10 minutes, cover and cook 20 minutes longer.   6 servings

DUMPLINGS

1½ cup flour
2 teaspoons baking powder
¾ teaspoon salt
2 tablespoons minced parsley
3 tablespoons margarine
¾ cup milk

1. In a medium bowl, combine flour, baking powder, salt and parsley. Blend in margarine with a pastry blender or fork until the mixture resembles coarse meal.

2. Add milk and mix well; if necessary, add more milk to make mixture hold together.

Teriyaki London Broil

Serve with Rice Pilaf and a crisp salad for an easy company dinner.

1 (2-pound) flank steak, fat trimmed
⅓ cup soy sauce
¼ cup vegetable oil
¼ cup water
¼ cup red wine vinegar
2 cloves garlic, chopped fine
4 drops Tabasco sauce
Freshly ground pepper

1. Place steak in a shallow baking dish. In a small bowl, combine remaining ingredients and pour marinade over steak. Cover and let stand 2 to 3 hours, turning steak several times.

2. Preheat broiler. Remove steak from marinade and place on a broiling pan. Broil steak 3 inches from heat, about 5 minutes per side. Season with freshly ground pepper. Cut in very thin slices, diagonally, across the grain. Transfer to a warmed platter and serve immediately.   4 servings

Slottstek (Royal Swedish Pot Roast)

A rich, dark gravy tenderizes this flavorful oven-simmered roast. Serve with boiled new potatoes.

2 tablespoons butter
2 tablespoons vegetable oil
1 medium onion, chopped
3 tablespoons flour
4 pounds boneless beef roast (round, rump, brisket or chuck)
1 tablespoon dark corn syrup
2 tablespoons white vinegar
2 cups BEEF STOCK
1 bay leaf
6 anchovies, washed and dried (optional)
1/4 teaspoon coarsely ground pepper

1. In a large Dutch oven, over medium heat, melt butter and oil. Sauté onion until soft, about 6 minutes. Remove from pan and set aside.

2. Dredge roast in flour and brown about 8 minutes on each side; remove roast and set aside. Reserve unused flour.

3. Preheat oven to 350°. Discard all but 1 tablespoon of oil. Add remaining flour and cook 2 minutes. Return meat and onion to pot; add all remaining ingredients. Bring to a boil on top of stove.

4. Cover Dutch oven and place in lower third of oven. Reduce heat so that liquid barely simmers, about 325°. Cook for 3 hours or until meat is tender.

5. Transfer the roast to a heated platter and cover with foil to keep warm. Skim off any oil from the top of gravy. Boil briskly, uncovered, for 5-10 minutes to reduce and thicken. Salt and pepper to taste. Pour into gravy bowl and serve with sliced roast. 4-6 servings

Eggplant Moussaka

A favorite for any eggplant lover, this dish is even better reheated the next day. Serve with French bread, a crisp green salad and a red wine.

1 medium onion, chopped
2 cloves garlic, minced
2 tablespoons olive or vegetable oil
1 1/2 pounds ground beef or lamb (or combination)
1 (8-ounce) can tomato sauce
1 (6-ounce) can tomato paste
1/3 cup dry red wine
1/4 cup chopped fresh parsley
1 teaspoon dried basil
1 teaspoon dried oregano
1 teaspoon sugar
1/4 teaspoon cinnamon
2 teaspoons salt
1/4 teaspoon freshly ground pepper
1 cup water
2 medium eggplants, peeled if desired
1/2 cup salad oil
1/4 cup butter or margarine
1/4 cup flour
2 cups milk, warmed
3 eggs, beaten
1 (16-ounce) carton ricotta cheese
1/4 teaspoon nutmeg
1/4 cup grated Parmesan cheese

1. To prepare meat sauce: In a large skillet, sauté onion and garlic in oil until onion is soft. Add the ground meat and brown; discard any excess oil. Add tomato sauce, tomato paste, wine, parsley, basil, oregano, sugar, cinnamon, salt, pepper and water. Simmer, uncovered, over low heat until sauce has thickened, about 20 minutes. Remove from heat.

2. While sauce is cooking, preheat oven to 350°. Cut eggplants into 1/2-inch thick slices; brush both sides with oil and place on baking sheets. Bake about 10 minutes. Eggplant will be partially cooked. Remove from oven and set aside.

3. To prepare ricotta sauce: In a medium saucepan, melt butter and blend in flour; gradually whisk in heated milk. Continue cooking, stirring con-

stantly until mixture is thick and smooth. Remove from heat and cool slightly. Stir in eggs, ricotta cheese and nutmeg; set aside.

4. Grease a large 12x18-inch baking pan. Layer meat sauce and eggplant into pan, beginning and ending with meat sauce. Pour ricotta sauce over the top and sprinkle with Parmesan. Bake for 1 hour, uncovered. Let stand 20 minutes before cutting.   8 servings

Greek Shish-Kabobs

Marinating the meat intensifies the flavor of this traditional Greek dish.

Marinade
1/2 cup oil
1/4 cup lemon juice
1 teaspoon garlic powder
1 teaspoon onion powder
1 teaspoon dried oregano
1/2 teaspoon dried basil
1/4 teaspoon mint, crushed
1/2 teaspoon salt
1/4 teaspoon pepper
Kabob
1 pound beef, sirloin or tender chuck steak
1 pound lamb, shoulder cut
4 small zucchini, cut into chunks
1 sweet red pepper, cut into 1-inch cubes
18 medium mushrooms

1. In a large bowl, mix together all marinade ingredients. Cut meat into 1 1/2-inch cubes and place in marinade.

2. Using individual skewers, alternate meat with vegetables. Place kabobs in pan and pour marinade over the top. Marinate for 5 minutes.

3. Preheat broiler. Remove kabobs from marinade and broil 5 to 7 minutes on each side; baste occasionally. Serve on rice cooked in chicken stock.

6 servings

Guemes Lamb Pie

This unusual dish was created by Dorothy Bird. It has a delightful combination of flavors.

Tomato Sauce
1 tablespoon olive oil
1 clove garlic, minced
¼ cup chopped onion
¼ cup sliced mushrooms
¼ cup red or green bell peppers
1 (16-ounce) can tomatoes, including juice
1 (6-ounce) can tomato paste
¼ cup fresh or 1 tablespoon dried basil
¼ cup fresh minced parsley
½ cup sliced ripe olives
1 bay leaf
Meat Layer
3 tablespoons olive oil
¼ cup chopped onion
1½ pounds ground lamb
1 cup cubed eggplant
1 small zucchini, sliced
½ cup pine nuts
½ cup raisins
1 teaspoon cinnamon
½ teaspoon allspice
½ teaspoon freshly ground pepper

Pasta Layer
1½ cups pasta, rigatoni or penne
2 cups grated sharp Cheddar cheese
3 eggs, beaten

1. To prepare tomato sauce: In a skillet, heat oil over medium heat. Sauté garlic, onion, mushrooms and peppers until onion is soft. Add remaining sauce ingredients and simmer, covered, for 30 minutes.

2. To prepare meat layer: In a Dutch oven, heat 1½ tablespoons oil over medium heat. Sauté onion until soft; add lamb and brown. Remove lamb and onion with a slotted spoon and set aside. Discard fat from pan. In same pan, heat remaining 1½ tablespoons oil over medium heat and sauté eggplant and zucchini. Add reserved lamb and remaining 5 ingredients. Mix well and set aside. Preheat oven to 350°.

3. To prepare pasta layer: In a large pot, cook pasta al dente, according to package directions. Drain and return to pot; add cheese and eggs. Toss to coat.

4. Grease a 4 or 5-quart baking dish. Layer pasta in bottom of pan; top with meat layer and cover with tomato sauce. Dish can be refrigerated or frozen at this time. Cover and bake, for 30 minutes, or 20 minutes longer, if dish has been refrigerated.   8 servings

Karageorges' Roast Leg of Lamb

If anyone knows how to prepare lamb, it is the Karageorges family on Orcas Island which, for many years ran a sheep ranch. Serve with our Asparagus Salad topped with Dijon Vinaigrette for a special spring meal.

1 (5-pound) leg of lamb
3 cloves garlic, peeled and slivered
1 large lemon
2 teaspoons dried oregano
Salt and coarsely ground pepper
1 cup water
6 baking potatoes, peeled

1. Preheat oven to 300°. Trim fat from lamb; place the lamb on a rack in a large roasting pan. Make incisions in the lamb and insert garlic slivers.

2. Cut lemon in half and rub surface of the lamb with lemon halves. Squeeze lemon over lamb, using all the juice. Sprinkle with oregano, salt and pepper.

3. Pour water in the bottom of the roasting pan. Make a loose foil tent and cover lamb; foil should not touch meat. Bake for 1 hour.

4. Pour off any oil. Add additional water, so that water totals approximately 1 cup. Quarter potatoes and place in water around meat. Remove foil and bake an additional hour or until lamb and potatoes are done. For rare lamb, meat thermometer will read 140°, for well-done, 175°.

5. Remove roasting pan from oven. Transfer lamb to a warm platter to rest for 20 minutes before carving. Remove potatoes to a serving bowl and cover to keep warm. Discard grease from pan juices and prepare a gravy, if desired.   6-8 servings

Stuffed Cabbage Rolls

This is a favorite recipe of a Decatur Island family. The combination of sauerkraut and sour cream makes it memorable.

1 large head cabbage
1 tablespoon vegetable oil
1/3 cup chopped onion
1 clove garlic, minced
1 egg, slightly beaten
1 pound lean ground beef
1 cup cooked rice
1/4 teaspoon allspice
1 teaspoon salt
1/4 teaspoon freshly ground pepper
1 (16-ounce) can sauerkraut, drained
2 (8-ounce) cans tomato sauce
Sour cream

1. Cut a circle around the core of the cabbage to loosen the leaves. Then drop leaves, one at a time, in a large pot of boiling salted water. Simmer leaves about 4 minutes or until leaves are soft enough to roll; drain and cool. To make rolling easier, cut away the thickest portion of the hard spine of the larger leaves.

2. In a small frying pan, heat oil over medium heat. Sauté onion and garlic until onion is soft. Remove from heat and set aside.

3. In a large mixing bowl, combine egg, beef, rice, sautéed onion and garlic and all seasonings; set aside.

4. Preheat oven to 350°. In a 13x9-inch greased baking pan, spread sauerkraut. Pour 1 can tomato sauce evenly over the top.

5. Stuff cabbage leaves with meat and rice mixture; place rolls seam side down on sauerkraut. Pour remaining can of tomato sauce over cabbage rolls. Cover and bake for 1 hour. Serve with sour cream.   6 servings

Bilbo's Chili Colorado

Bilbo's Restaurant in Eastsound on Orcas Island serves authentic Mexican and Southwestern cuisine using only the freshest of ingredients. The comfortable festive atmosphere is enhanced by a lovely courtyard with a grape arbor and adobe walls.

1 (3-4 pound) pork shoulder roast
3 tablespoons vegetable oil
1 large yellow onion, diced
3-4 cloves garlic, minced
1 tablespoon pure red chili peppers*
1 tablespoon pure red chili powder*
1 tablespoon coarse ground Mexican oregano
1/4 cup flour
3 cups stock or water
1 teaspoon salt
Cinnamon stick (optional)
Spanish rice
Refried beans
Flour tortillas
Lime wedges

1. Trim fat from pork and discard. Cut meat into 1/2-inch chunks, set aside.

2. In a large skillet, over medium-high, heat oil and brown pork in two separate batches. Remove meat from pan with a slotted spoon. Pour remaining pan juices into a bowl; set aside.

3. Add 1 tablespoon oil to skillet, over medium-high heat, sauté onion and garlic until onion is soft. Return meat to pan; add chili peppers, chili powder and oregano. Blend in flour and stir for 2 minutes. Add reserved pan juices and stock to pan and bring to a boil. If sauce seems too thick add water to thin to desired consistency. Add salt and cinnamon. Cover and simmer until tender, about 1 hour.

4. Serve on a warm platter with rice, beans and tortillas. Garnish with lime wedges.   6 servings

*Available in the foreign food section of most supermarkets.

Carbonara San Juan

Pesto sauce adds flair to this pasta dish. Serve with our Sautéed Zucchini with Basil, a green salad and French bread.

1/2 pound mild Italian pork sausage, casings removed
8 ounces spaghetti pasta

2 tablespoons olive oil
2 tablespoons PESTO SAUCE
3 eggs, beaten
1/2 cup chopped fresh parsley
1/3 cup grated Parmesan cheese
1/2 teaspoon salt
1/4 teaspoon freshly ground pepper, to taste
Parmesan cheese

1. In a large skillet, over medium high heat, fry crumbled sausage until golden brown, about 10 minutes. Be sure sausage is cooked through. Drain sausage and set aside; discard grease.

2. While sausage is browning, in a large pot cook pasta al dente, according to package directions. Drain and return to pot. Add olive oil and Pesto Sauce and toss to coat pasta. Add sausage to pasta and keep warm over low heat.

3. Add beaten eggs, parsley, Parmesan, salt and pepper to pasta. Toss gently to blend. Transfer to heated platter and serve with additional Parmesan.

4-6 servings

Fettucine with Artichokes

An enticing combination of bacon, mushrooms and artichoke hearts makes this an attractive and savory dish.

8 slices bacon, sliced into ½-inch pieces
3 tablespoons butter or margarine
2 cloves garlic, minced
3 green onions, sliced (tops removed)
2 cups sliced mushrooms
2 medium tomatoes, peeled, seeded and chopped
1 (8-ounce) can artichoke hearts, drained and sliced
⅓ cup sour cream
½ cup light cream
8 ounces fettucine
2 tablespoons olive oil
2 tablespoons PESTO SAUCE (optional)
1 tablespoon minced fresh parsley
½ teaspoon dried thyme
½ teaspoon dried oregano
Salt and freshly ground pepper
⅓ cup freshly grated Parmesan cheese

1. In a large frying pan, cook bacon over medium heat until done but not crisp. Remove bacon and set aside; discard grease.

2. In the same frying pan, melt butter over medium heat. Add garlic, onions, mushrooms and tomatoes; sauté until onions are soft. Add artichokes, bacon, sour cream and light cream. Heat through; do not boil.

3. While vegetables are sautéing, in a large pot cook pasta al dente, according to package directions. Drain and return to pot. Add olive oil and Pesto Sauce, if desired, and toss to coat pasta. Toss with parsley, thyme, oregano, salt and pepper.

4. Pour vegetable mixture into pasta pot and toss with Parmesan. Transfer to a heated platter and serve immediately.   4 servings

Smoked Ham with Spinach Pasta

An appealing combination of flavor and color.

1 (12-ounce) package spinach pasta
2 tablespoons vegetable oil
$1/4$ cup butter or margarine
12 ounces smoked ham or proscuitto, cut into julienne strips
$1/2$ cup sliced mushrooms
1 (10-ounce) package frozen spinach, thawed and well drained or $1/2$ pound fresh
    spinach, washed, drained and chopped
$1/2$ cup ricotta cheese
$1/4$ cup finely chopped walnuts or whole pine nuts
$1/2$ teaspoon dried marjoram
$1 1/4$ cups light cream
Salt and freshly ground pepper, to taste
Parmesan cheese

1. In a large pot, cook pasta al dente, according to package directions. Drain, return to pot and add 2 tablespoons oil; toss to coat. Cover to keep warm.

2. In a large skillet, over medium-high heat, melt butter. Sauté ham or proscuitto and mushrooms until ham is golden brown, about 5 minutes. Remove and set aside.

3. Add drained spinach to skillet and sauté until cooked through. Add reserved ham and mushrooms to spinach. Keep warm over low heat.

4. In a small bowl, combine ricotta, nuts, marjoram and cream. Pour into ham and spinach mixture and heat through. Add all ingredients to pasta and toss gently to blend. Salt and pepper to taste. Transfer to a warm serving platter. Sprinkle with Parmesan and serve immediately.   4-6 servings

Chicken and Eggplant

This colorful dish is reminiscent of ratatouille. Serve it with a combination of white and wild rice for an attractive entree.

2 tablespoons butter or margarine
1/4 cup flour
1 (3-pound) broiler-fryer, cut into serving pieces
Salt and pepper
2 cloves garlic, minced
1 medium onion, chopped
1/2 green bell pepper, chopped into 1/2-inch cubes
1/2 red bell pepper, chopped into 1/2-inch cubes (optional)
1 large eggplant, cut into 1-inch cubes
1 cup sliced mushrooms
1 (16-ounce) can tomatoes, diced
1/2 teaspoon each dried basil, oregano and thyme
1 bay leaf
1 tablespoon fresh minced parsley
Salt and pepper, to taste
1/3 cup dry white wine
Parmesan cheese

1. In a large skillet, heat butter and brown floured chicken. Season with salt and pepper. Remove chicken from pan; set aside.

2. Add garlic, onion, bell peppers, eggplant and mushrooms to skillet and sauté until vegetables are slightly softened. Discard remaining oil. Add remaining 6 ingredients; bring to a boil and simmer for 5 minutes.

3. Return chicken pieces to sauce; cover and simmer for about 40 minutes or until chicken is done. Turn chicken occasionally to coat with sauce. Turn onto heated serving dish and garnish with Parmesan.   4-6 servings

Chicken and Shrimp Marsala

An enticing combination in a robust tomato sauce. With our Greek Salad and freshly baked French bread, this makes a special meal.

1/4 cup butter or margarine
1/4 cup chopped green onions or shallots
1 clove garlic, minced
1 teaspoon salt
1/4 teaspoon pepper
6 chicken breast halves skinned, boned and halved
1/2 cup flour
1 (8-ounce) can tomato sauce
1/4 cup Marsala wine
1 teaspoon dried basil
2 tablespoons chopped fresh parsley
2 tablespoons butter
2 cups fresh or frozen cooked shrimp, deveined
Parsley

1. In a large skillet, over medium heat, melt butter and sauté onions and garlic, about 3 minutes; do not burn garlic. With a slotted spoon, remove mixture to a small bowl and set aside.

2. Salt and pepper chicken breasts and lightly dust with flour. In butter remaining in skillet, brown chicken over medium-high heat until golden on all sides. Remove from skillet and arrange pieces in a baking-serving dish. Chicken can be refrigerated at this time, if desired.

3. Preheat oven to 325°. Deglaze skillet by adding tomato sauce, wine, basil, parsley and reserved onion mixture. Bring to a boil and remove from heat. Spoon sauce over chicken and cover with foil. Bake for 25-35 minutes or until juices run clear when pierced with a fork. Bake 15-20 minutes, longer if chicken was refrigerated.

4. While chicken is baking, heat 2 tablespoons butter in a skillet and add shrimp. Sauté over low heat for 2 to 3 minutes or until heated through. Sprinkle shrimp over chicken and garnish with parsley.   6 servings

Chicken Piccata

An elegant and easy company dinner. Veal can be substituted for the chicken.

    4 chicken breast halves, skinned, boned and halved
    ¼ cup flour
    ½ teaspoon salt
    3 tablespoons butter
    1 clove garlic, thinly sliced
    ¼ cup dry vermouth or dry white wine
    2 tablespoons fresh lemon juice
    ½ lemon, thinly sliced
    2 tablespoons capers
    2 tablespoons fresh minced parsley

1. Place chicken between 2 pieces of waxed paper and pound with mallet to a thickness of ¼-inch.

2. In a plastic bag, mix flour and salt and coat chicken. In a large skillet, heat butter over medium-high heat. Cook garlic until brown and discard. Quickly sauté chicken until browned, about 2 minutes each side. Remove to warm platter and cover.

3. Deglaze pan with vermouth and lemon juice. Return chicken to pan and heat through; top with lemon slices.

4. Transfer chicken to serving plates and top with sauce. Garnish with capers and parsley. Serve immediately.   4 servings

Chicken with Raspberry Vinegar

Raspberry Vinegar adds the flavor of summer to this dish. It is available at gourmet shops or you can make your own when raspberries are at their best in July.

2 tablespoons butter
6 chicken breast halves, skinned and cut in half
¼ cup flour
Salt and ground pepper
1 clove garlic, minced
2 shallots or 2 green onions, chopped fine
1½ cups sliced mushrooms
¼ cup RASPBERRY VINEGAR
½ cup CHICKEN STOCK
½ cup heavy cream
Salt and ground pepper, to taste
Mint leaves

1. In a large skillet, heat butter. Dust chicken lightly with flour and season with salt and pepper. Sauté chicken on both sides until golden. Remove from pan and set aside.

2. Remove all but 1 tablespoon of oil from pan, sauté garlic, onion and mushrooms until onion is soft. Discard remaining oil. Deglaze pan by adding Raspberry Vinegar and Chicken Stock. Add chicken, cover and simmer about 30 minutes or until chicken juices run clear when pierced with a fork. Remove to heated platter and cover with foil to keep warm.

3. Bring sauce to a boil and simmer until sauce thickens. Add cream and reduce again, about 4 minutes. Salt and pepper to taste. Serve chicken on rice; pour sauce over chicken. Garnish with mint leaves.   4-6 servings

Chicken with Tarragon-Lemon Cream

A tart tarragon and lemon cream sauce complements this chicken dish.

2 tablespoons butter or margarine
4 chicken breast halves, cut in half
¼ cup flour
½ teaspoon salt
¼ teaspoon freshly ground pepper
1 clove garlic, minced
4 green onions or shallots, thinly sliced (tops removed)
1 cup sliced mushrooms
½ cup CHICKEN STOCK
¼ cup dry white wine
2 tablespoons lemon juice
½ cup heavy cream
½ teaspoon dried tarragon leaves

1. Preheat oven to 350°. In a large frying pan, melt butter over medium-high heat. Brown floured chicken and season with salt and pepper. Remove chicken from pan and place in a shallow baking dish. Cover and bake for 30 minutes.

2. Remove all but 1 tablespoon of butter from pan. Sauté garlic, onion and mushrooms in remaining butter until soft. Deglaze pan with Chicken Stock, wine and lemon juice. Simmer to reduce liquid, about 5 minutes.

3. Add cream and tarragon to wine mixture; simmer for 5 minutes to reduce. Do not boil.

4. Pour sauce over chicken. Bake uncovered for 10 minutes. Serve with rice or new potatoes.   4 servings

Crispy Parmesan Chicken

Served warm or cold, this is great to take along on a picnic with our Pasta Salad.

1 cup crushed saltine crackers
1/4 cup grated Parmesan cheese
2 tablespoons minced fresh parsley
1/2 teaspoon dried oregano
1/2 teaspoon dried basil
1/2 teaspoon dried thyme
1/4 teaspoon paprika
1 teaspoon salt
1/4 teaspoon ground fresh pepper
1 (3-pound) broiler-fryer, cut into serving pieces
1/2 cup light cream or buttermilk
1/3 cup vegetable oil

1. Preheat oven to 350°. In a plastic bag, combine saltines, Parmesan and all seasonings. Dip chicken pieces in cream or buttermilk and shake in bag with seasonings. Place skin side up in a greased large baking dish. Bake for 30 minutes.

2. Sprinkle chicken pieces with oil and continue baking 30 more minutes or until chicken is browned and juices run clear when pierced with a fork. Serve warm or cold.
4 servings

Grilled Chicken Breasts with Peanut Sauce

Tender marinated chicken breasts are served with an unusual peanut sauce.

3 whole chicken breasts, boned and skinned
1/2 cup vegetable oil
3 tablespoons lemon juice
3 tablespoons soy sauce
4 tablespoons brown sugar
1 clove garlic, minced
1/8 teaspoon ground red pepper
1/4 teaspoon freshly ground pepper
PEANUT SAUCE (see below)

1. Between two pieces of waxed paper, place breast fillets. With a mallet, pound gently to flatten to a thickness of 3/8-inch. Cut each fillet in half, making 12 pieces. Place in a shallow baking dish.

2. In a medium bowl, prepare marinade by combining oil, lemon juice, soy sauce, sugar and seasonings. Pour over chicken; cover and refrigerate. Marinate for 2-3 hours.

3. While chicken is marinating, prepare Peanut Sauce and set aside in a small serving bowl.

4. Preheat broiler. Remove chicken from marinade and arrange on broiler rack 5 inches away from heat source. Cook approximately 5 minutes on each side. Brush with marinade at least once; do not overcook.

5. Remove to a warm serving platter and serve with Peanut Sauce.

6 servings

PEANUT SAUCE

1/3 cup water
2/3 cup crunchy peanut butter
1 tablespoon soy sauce
1/4 cup lemon juice

2 tablespoons minced onion
1 clove garlic, minced
1/2 teaspoon crushed chili peppers
1/2 teaspoon coriander

In a saucepan, bring water to a boil. Add remaining ingredients. Reduce heat and simmer for 5 minutes, stirring occasionally. 1 1/4 cups

Homemade Noodles with Chicken

There is nothing like the taste of Grandma Cora's homemade pasta. These noodles need to be prepared several hours before serving time to dry thoroughly before cutting. The dried uncooked noodles freeze well in plastic bags.

2 large eggs, beaten
1 teaspoon salt
¼ cup light cream or milk
1¾ cups flour
1½-2 pounds chicken pieces (wings, thighs) or 1 whole chicken
4 quarts water
½ medium onion
1 stalk celery
1 sprig parsley
1 clove garlic
2 teaspoons salt
¼ teaspoon coarsely ground pepper

1. To prepare noodles: In a large bowl, combine eggs, salt and cream. Slowly add flour, blending with a fork until a stiff ball is formed; add additional flour if needed.

2. Dust a board with flour; knead dough until smooth. Cover with clean towel and set aside for 20 minutes. Dough will relax and be easier to roll.

3. Roll dough very thin on floured surface. Allow to dry, about 2 hours. When top surface is dry, cut dough into 4 equal strips and turn to dry underside, about 30 minutes.

4. Layer noodle strips on top of each other, dusting each layer with flour to prevent sticking. With a sharp knife, cut across strips making ⅛-inch wide noodles.

5. To prepare chicken: While noodles are drying, combine remaining ingredients in a kettle. Bring to a boil; skim off froth. Reduce heat and simmer for 1 hour or until chicken can be easily removed from bones. Remove chicken from broth. Discard all bones and skin; set chicken meat aside. Remove vegetables from broth with a slotted spoon and discard vegetables.

6. Bring broth to a rolling boil. There should be approximately 2½ quarts of broth, add water, if necessary. Drop noodles into boiling broth, stirring to separate. Boil until noodles are tender, about 20 minutes. Stir in reserved chicken and heat through. Salt and pepper to taste.   4 servings

Honey-Ginger Chicken

Yuriko Bullock of Orcas Island has a long history of professional cooking. Her catering service specializes in an eclectic mixture of Oriental and Northwest cuisine. She developed this dish for a "picnic-style" wedding. Serve it with her Stir-Fried Vegetables with Black Bean Sauce.

½ cup soy sauce
3 tablespoons dry sherry
2 tablespoons honey
2 tablespoons Worcestershire sauce
3 tablespoons finely minced fresh ginger
5-6 cloves garlic, finely minced
1 (3-pound) broiler-fryer, cut into serving pieces

1. In a large bowl, combine all ingredients except chicken. Add chicken pieces and toss to coat. Marinate 1½ to 2 hours, turn chicken pieces occasionally.

2. Preheat oven to 350°. Remove chicken from marinade and place in a greased 13x9-inch baking dish. Bake for 50 minutes or until juices run clear when pierced with a fork; baste occasionally. Remove from pan and serve with rice.   4 servings

Garlic Chicken

This chicken dish is a longstanding favorite at La Petite Restaurant in Anacortes on Fidalgo Island. If you have time on your way to the San Juans, stop and enjoy a fine European dinner.

3 whole chicken breasts, halved, skinned and boned
½ teaspoon salt
¼ teaspoon freshly ground pepper
4½ tablespoons Dijon mustard
3½ tablespoons butter
8 cloves garlic, finely chopped
½ cup CHICKEN STOCK
1 (16-ounce) package bow-tie pasta
1½ tablespoons butter
2 tablespoons finely chopped parsley
1½ teaspoons finely chopped fresh basil
1 cup heavy cream
1 teaspoon salt
¼ teaspoon freshly ground pepper
⅓ cup freshly grated Parmesan cheese

1. Put chicken breasts between plastic wrap and pound to a ⅜-inch thickness. Lightly salt and pepper chicken. Coat chicken with mustard and set aside for 10 minutes.

2. Preheat oven to 350°. In a large skillet, over medium-high heat, melt 2½ tablespoons butter. Pan must be large enough to accommodate chicken without crowding. You may have to cook chicken in two batches. Quickly brown chicken on both sides. Remove pan from heat and transfer chicken to an oven-proof platter. Place in oven for approximately 10 minutes, or until chicken is done.

3. In chicken skillet, melt 1 tablespoon butter over medium heat. Sauté garlic about 2 minutes; do not allow to brown. Add stock and simmer until liquid reduces by half.

4. In a large pot, cook pasta al dente, according to package directions; drain in colander. While pasta is draining, melt 1½ tablespoons butter in pot. Add pasta, 1½ tablespoons parsley and basil to pot. Cover with lid to keep warm.

5. While pasta is cooking, add cream, remaining parsley, salt and pepper to reduced chicken stock. Stirring frequently, simmer to reduce until sauce coats the back of a spoon.

6. Transfer pasta to a warm platter and sprinkle with Parmesan. Place chicken on top of pasta and spoon garlic sauce over chicken.   6 servings

Summer Chicken

Dawn entered this recipe in the 1982 Washington State Chicken Cooking Contest and was surprised with a win. The judges loved the lively lemon sauce and so will your family.

4 tablespoons butter
1 (3-pound) broiler-fryer, cut into serving pieces
1 pound small new red potatoes
Salt and freshly ground pepper
2 tablespoons fresh lemon juice
4 green onions, (with tops) thinly sliced
1 (10-ounce) package frozen peas or fresh sugar snap peas, cut if desired
2 tablespoons chopped fresh parsley
1 cup sour cream or yogurt
1/4 cup milk
1 teaspoon dried thyme
Salt and pepper, to taste

1. In a large frying pan, melt butter over medium heat. Add chicken and potatoes and brown on all sides. Season with salt and pepper. Sprinkle chicken with lemon juice. Cover and simmer over low heat for 30 minutes.

2. Sprinkle onions, peas and parsley over chicken. Cover and cook 10 more minutes or until chicken juices run clear when pierced with a fork and potatoes are done. Remove chicken, potatoes and peas to a heated platter; cover to keep warm.

3. Discard remaining oil. Add sour cream, milk, thyme, salt and pepper. Simmer over low heat about 5 minutes or until sauce is heated through, stirring occasionally; do not boil. Pour sauce over chicken and potatoes and serve immediately.   4 servings

Pasta Primavera

Gardens thrive in our mild Northwest climate. When yours is full of fresh vegetables, prepare this attractive and delicious entree.

1 pound fettucine
4 tablespoons olive oil
2 tablespoons PESTO SAUCE
2 tablespoons butter
3 cloves garlic, minced
1½ cups sliced asparagus
½ head cauliflower, broken into flowerets
1 bunch broccoli, broken into flowerets, stems peeled and sliced
1½ cups snow peas
2 zucchini, sliced
1 cup sliced mushrooms
¼ cup chopped fresh or 2 teaspoons dry basil
1 cup heavy cream
½ cup CHICKEN STOCK
3 green onions, thinly chopped
2 tablespoons chopped fresh parsley
½ cup freshly grated Parmesan cheese
Salt and freshly ground pepper, to taste

1. In a large pot, cook pasta al dente, according to package directions. Drain and return to pot. Add 2 tablespoons olive oil and Pesto Sauce; toss to coat pasta. Cover to keep warm.

2. In a large frying pan or wok over medium-high, heat remaining 2 tablespoons oil and butter. Stir in garlic, asparagus, cauliflower, broccoli, peas, zucchini and mushrooms. Stir-fry for 8 minutes or until vegetables are tender-crisp. Cover for 2 minutes to shorten cooking time, if desired.

3. Add basil, cream, and Chicken Stock to vegetables. Simmer about 4 minutes or until liquid thickens slightly. Stir in onions and parsley. Add vegetable mixture and Parmesan to pasta and toss gently. Salt and pepper to taste.

4. Turn onto serving platter and garnish with additional Parmesan, if desired. Serve immediately.   6 servings

Potato Egg Pie

Olympic Lights, a San Juan Island bed and breakfast inn, serves this favorite recipe as an entree to family and friends. This comfortable guest home sits in an open meadow with a panoramic view of the water and the Olympic Mountain Range.

2 tablespoons butter or margarine
1 tablespoon flour
1/2 teaspoon salt
1/8 teaspoon freshly ground pepper
1/2 cup milk
3 cups seasoned mashed potatoes
4 hard-cooked eggs
2 tablespoons crumbled, crisp bacon
2 tablespoons minced fresh parsley
1/4 cup grated Cheddar cheese
2 tablespoons milk

1. In a small saucepan, over medium heat, melt butter. Blend in flour, salt and pepper. Gradually whisk in milk, stirring constantly until mixture thickens and bubbles. Remove from heat and set aside.

2. Preheat oven to 400°. Line the bottom and sides of a greased 9-inch pie plate with half the potatoes. Slice eggs and arrange in potato shell. Top with bacon, parsley, cheese and reserved white sauce. Cover with remaining potatoes.

3. Brush top of pie with 2 tablespoons milk. Bake for 20 minutes or until top is nicely browned. 4-6 servings

Pizza with French Bread Crust

A crispy homemade French bread crust makes this pizza special. It is sure to please your crowd.

Pizza Crust
1 package active yeast, 2½ teaspoons
1 cup warm water (about 110°)
2 tablespoons olive oil
1 teaspoon sugar
1 teaspoon salt
2 cups flour
Sauce
1 tablespoon olive oil
2 cloves garlic, minced
½ medium onion, chopped
1 (8-ounce) can tomato sauce
1 (6-ounce) can tomato paste
½ teaspoon dried oregano
1 teaspoon salt
¼ teaspoon freshly ground pepper
Topping
¼ pound Canadian bacon, sliced
½ green pepper, sliced or chopped
½ pound fresh mushrooms, sliced
1 small zucchini, sliced
1 (16-ounce) can ripe black olives, sliced
1 (12-ounce) package mozzarella cheese, grated
¼ cup Parmesan cheese

1. To prepare crust: In a large mixing bowl or food processor, dissolve yeast in warm water. Allow to proof for 3 minutes; stir in oil. Add sugar and salt to yeast mixture. Add flour, 1 cup at a time, until dough begins to ball and pull away from the side of the bowl. Knead until dough is smooth and elastic. Add additional flour, if necessary.

2. Place dough in a greased bowl; turn over to grease top. Cover with plastic wrap or a damp towel. Let rise in warm (80°) place until dough doubles, about 1 hour.

3. Prepare sauce while dough is rising: In a saucepan, heat oil over medium heat. Sauté garlic and onion until onion is soft. Add tomato sauce, to-

mato paste, oregano, salt and pepper. Simmer over low heat about 30 minutes. Remove from heat and set aside.

4. Preheat oven to 425°. After dough has risen, punch down and turn onto lightly floured board. Knead to squeeze out air bubbles. With a rolling pin, roll dough into a circle and place on pizza pan that has been greased and sprinkled with corn meal. It may be necessary to roll dough again on the pan.

5. Spread sauce on pizza dough and top with remaining ingredients. (At this point pizza may be covered tightly with foil and frozen for later use.) Bake on the lowest rack for 20 minutes. Allow to set for 5 minutes before cutting.

1 large pizza

Plum Sauce

A Shaw Island family enjoys this versatile sauce on grilled beef, poultry or lamb. It also makes a delicious Plum-Glazed Chicken in the oven.

2 tablespoons butter or margarine
2 medium Walla Walla onions, chopped
2 tablespoons minced shallots or leeks
1 clove garlic, minced
1 cup CHICKEN STOCK
3 cups pitted and quartered Italian plums
1 teaspoon fresh rosemary
1½ cups dry red wine
½ teaspoon salt
¼ teaspoon freshly ground pepper

1. In a large skillet, over medium heat, melt butter and sauté onion and garlic until soft. Add stock and simmer 15 minutes to reduce.

2. Add remaining ingredients and simmer to reduce and thicken. Cover and refrigerate remaining sauce. Use as a basting sauce for grilled meats.

3 cups

To prepare PLUM-GLAZED CHICKEN in the oven: Preheat oven to 350°. Place chicken pieces, skin-side up, in a shallow greased baking dish. Spoon Plum Sauce over chicken pieces. Cover and bake for 40 minutes. Remove cover, baste chicken and continue baking 20 minutes more or until chicken juices run clear when pierced with a fork. Discard any excess fat. Serve any remaining sauce at the table.

Basil Pesto Sauce

Make this delicious pesto in August when basil is garden-fresh. It can be used to flavor soups, sauces or vegetables. To make a quick Fettucine Alfredo, cook any pasta and add a thawed pesto cube or two, butter, cream and sprinkle with Parmesan.

    5 garlic cloves, peeled
    3 cups packed fresh basil leaves, stems removed
    ½ cup pine nuts
    ¾ cup freshly grated Parmesan cheese
    ⅔ cup olive oil

1. In a blender or food processor, mince garlic. Add basil, a little at a time, and mince. Add pine nuts and cheese and mince.

2. While machine is running, gradually pour in oil; mix until smooth. If mixture seems too thick, add more olive oil.

3. Cover and refrigerate for up to one week. Pesto can be stored in refrigerator for as long as 2 months, if ¼-inch of olive oil is always left on the top. Pesto may also be stored effectively by freezing in ice cube trays. When the cubes are frozen, transfer them to freezer bags for future use.   2 cups

Spinach Pesto Sauce

Who could ever tire of Basil Pesto? If you do, try this spinach variation from Elaine Anderson.

1 clove garlic, peeled
2 cups chopped fresh spinach, washed and stemmed
1/2 cup chopped fresh parsley
1/4 cup grated Parmesan cheese
1 teaspoon dried basil
1/3 cup walnut halves
1/2 teaspoon salt
1/4 teaspoon freshly ground pepper
3/4 cup olive oil

1. In a blender or food processor, mince garlic. Add spinach, a little at a time and mince. Add remaining ingredients, except oil.

2. While machine is running, gradually pour in oil and mix until smooth. If mixture seems too thick, add more oil.

3. Cover and refrigerate or freeze as you would our Basil Pesto Sauce.

2 cups

Vegetables

MATT BROWN   *Island Cove*

Braised Green Beans

Many gardeners in the San Juans grow green beans and pick them fresh for dinner. In this recipe, tender-crisp whole beans are served in a savory herb sauce.

1 pound fresh or frozen green beans
2-3 tablespoons olive oil
2 cloves garlic, minced
¾ cup chopped onion
1 cup sliced fresh mushrooms
2 medium tomatoes, peeled, seeded and coarsely chopped
1 teaspoon dried oregano
1 teaspoon dried thyme
1 teaspoon salt
Freshly ground pepper, to taste
Parmesan cheese

1. Remove ends from fresh clean beans. In a large pot, bring 4 cups of water to a boil; add beans and cook until tender-crisp, about 8 minutes. Drain and rinse under cold water; set aside.

2. While beans are cooking, heat oil in a large skillet over medium heat. Sauté garlic, onion and mushrooms, until onion is soft. Add tomatoes, oregano, thyme, salt and pepper; bring to a boil. Reduce heat; partially cover and simmer until liquid thickens and reduces, about 20 minutes.

3. Stir in beans, cover and simmer for 10 more minutes or until beans are heated through. Garnish with Parmesan cheese and serve.   4 servings

Green Lasagne

Green lasagne is a traditional and sumptuous favorite at Dawn's family gatherings.

1½ pounds fresh flat Italian beans, or 2 (10-ounce) packages frozen beans
4 medium potatoes
20 ounces lasagne pasta, broken into pieces
⅓ cup olive oil
⅓ cup PESTO SAUCE
⅓ cup chopped fresh parsley
½ cup grated Parmesan cheese
Salt and freshly ground pepper, to taste
Parmesan cheese

1. In a medium saucepan, steam beans until tender-crisp, 15 minutes for fresh and 8 minutes for frozen. Beans should be bright green. Drain and rinse with cold water; set aside.

2. While beans are steaming, boil potatoes in a large saucepan with enough water to cover. Cook until tender, about 15 minutes; drain. When cool, peel and slice; set aside.

3. While potatoes are cooking, cook pasta al dente, according to package directions. Drain and return to cooking pot. Add olive oil and Pesto Sauce; toss to coat. Add potatoes, beans, parsley and Parmesan. Salt and pepper to taste. Pour into a 13x9-inch baking dish. (Lasagne may be covered and refrigerated at this time.)

4. Bake, covered, at 350° for 30 minutes; if refrigerated bake an additional 20 minutes. Toss before serving; add additional olive oil if desired. Garnish with Parmesan.   10-12 servings

Eggplant Parmesan

Eggplant is baked rather than fried in this classic recipe.

  1 tablespoon olive oil
  2 cloves garlic, minced
  1 teaspoon dried basil
  ½ teaspoon dried oregano
  2 cups diced and peeled tomatoes, fresh or canned
  1 (8-ounce) can tomato sauce
  Salt and freshly ground pepper, to taste
  1 large or 2 medium eggplants, ends trimmed
  ⅓ cup vegetable oil
  2 cups shredded mozzarella cheese
  ½ cup grated Parmesan cheese

1. In a saucepan, heat oil over low heat and sauté garlic until golden; do not burn. Add herbs, tomatoes, tomato sauce, salt and pepper. Bring to a boil, reduce heat and simmer, uncovered, for 30 minutes; stirring occasionally.

2. Preheat oven to 450°. While sauce is simmering, peel eggplant, if desired, and cut into ½-inch slices. Brush both sides lightly with oil. Place in single layer on a cookie sheet and bake for 10 minutes.

3. Reduce oven heat to 350°. Pour ½ cup sauce in the bottom of a greased shallow 1½-quart casserole. Layer with one-half of eggplant; top with 1 cup sauce; sprinkle with 1 cup mozzarella cheese and ¼ cup Parmesan cheese; repeat layers. Cover and bake for 20 minutes; uncover and bake 10 minutes more, or until bubbly.

4-6 servings

Broccoli with Lemon and Parmesan

Lemon perks up the flavor of this broccoli dish.

> 1 large bunch broccoli, broken into flowerets and stems peeled and sliced
> DIJON MAYONNAISE (see below – optional)
> ¼ cup butter or margarine
> 3 tablespoons fresh lemon juice
> 3 tablespoons fresh grated Parmesan cheese
> Salt and pepper, to taste

1. In a large pot, cook broccoli in 2 inches of boiling water until fork-tender, about 8 minutes. Drain and return broccoli to pan.
2. While broccoli is cooking, prepare Dijon Mayonnaise, if desired.
3. Add butter to broccoli in warm pan, allowing butter to melt. Add lemon juice, Parmesan, salt and pepper; stir to coat broccoli. Remove to warm serving dish. Serve with Dijon Mayonnaise, if desired.   6 servings

DIJON MAYONNAISE

> ½ cup mayonnaise
> 1 teaspoon Dijon mustard

In a small bowl, combine mayonnaise and mustard. Pour into small serving bowl.

Carrots with Horseradish Sauce

This dish is a colorful accompaniment to a simple meat entree.

> 8 medium carrots, peeled and cut lengthwise into narrow strips
> ½ cup mayonnaise
> 1 tablespoon butter, softened
> 1 tablespoon horseradish
> 1 tablespoon minced fresh parsley
> ½ teaspoon salt
> Freshly ground pepper

1. In a medium pot, cook carrots in boiling water, about 10 minutes or until fork-tender. Rinse in cold water and arrange carrots in greased shallow baking dish.

2. Preheat oven to 375°. While carrots are cooking, combine in a small bowl: mayonnaise, butter, horseradish, parsley, salt and pepper. Spoon sauce over carrots. Bake, uncovered, for 15 minutes. Remove from oven and serve.

4-6 servings

Brussels Sprouts with Red Peppers and Capers

The combination of color and the lively flavor of lemon and capers distinguishes this tasty dish.

    1 pound Brussels sprouts, trimmed and washed
    2 tablespoons butter
    1 clove garlic, minced
    1 large red bell pepper, cut into strips
    1 tablespoon fresh lemon juice
    1 tablespoon capers

1. In a medium saucepan, cook Brussels sprouts in 2 inches of boiling water, until sprouts are fork tender. Drain and return to saucepan.

2. While sprouts are cooking, melt butter in a medium skillet; sauté garlic and bell pepper until tender. Add Brussels sprouts, lemon juice and capers; sauté until heated through. Transfer to a serving bowl.   4-6 servings

Sesame Red Cabbage and Pea Pods

This unusual and appealing combination comes to us from Barkley's of La Conner where Chef Michael Hood is known for his innovative cuisine.

GARLIC BUTTER (see below)
2 pounds red cabbage, cut into 1-inch squares
½ cup CHICKEN STOCK
Salt and freshly ground pepper, to taste
6 ounces fresh or frozen Chinese pea pods, snapped and strung
3 tablespoons sesame oil

1. Prepare Garlic Butter and set aside.
2. In a large skillet, over high heat, stir-fry cabbage in Chicken Stock. Add salt and pepper and cook until cabbage is tender-crisp.
3. Add pea pods to cabbage (frozen pea pods should be unthawed). Cover pan for 3-4 minutes or until pea pods are tender. Add Garlic Butter and sesame oil to cabbage mixture and toss gently; serve immediately.

6-8 servings

GARLIC BUTTER

1 cube (4 ounces) butter, at room temperature
5 cloves garlic, minced
1 teaspoon Worcestershire sauce
1 tablespoon Cognac
2 tablespoons chopped fresh parsley

In a small bowl, combine all ingredients.

Parsleyed New Potatoes

Simplicity at its best!

> 2 pounds small new potatoes, scrubbed
> 6 tablespoons butter
> 2 teaspoons lemon juice
> 2 tablespoons minced fresh parsley
> 1 teaspoon dill weed (optional)
> Salt and freshly ground pepper, to taste

1. In a medium pot, cook potatoes in boiling water until fork tender, about 10 minutes; do not overcook. Drain and set aside.

2. In same pot, melt butter over medium heat; add potatoes, lemon juice, parsley, dill weed, salt and pepper. Sauté until heated through

6 servings

Parmesan Oven-Fried Potatoes

A crispy favorite that goes with many fish and meat dishes.

> 6 medium potatoes, peeled
> ¼ cup butter or margarine
> ¼ cup grated Parmesan cheese
> Salt and freshly ground pepper, to taste

1. Preheat oven to 375°. Slice potatoes ¼-inch thick; separate slices and place on towels to dry.

2. In a jelly roll pan, melt butter in oven; do not burn. Remove pan from oven and arrange potato slices. Sprinkle with Parmesan, salt and pepper.

3. Bake uncovered for 20 minutes; turn slices with spatula and continue cooking for 20 minutes more or until crispy brown. Serve immediately.

4-6 servings

Frosted Cauliflower

This dish makes a lovely presentation at the table.

    1 medium head cauliflower, cleaned and trimmed
    ½ cup mayonnaise
    2 teaspoons Dijon mustard
    ½ teaspoon curry powder
    ¾ cup grated Cheddar cheese

1. In a large pot, steam whole cauliflower for 12 minutes in 2 inches salted water. Remove with slotted spoon and place in a greased shallow baking dish.

2. Preheat oven to 375°. While cauliflower is cooking, combine remaining ingredients in a small bowl. Frost the cauliflower head with mayonnaise mixture. Bake uncovered for 10 minutes or until golden. Serve immediately.

4 servings

Fresh Sautéed Vegetables

The flavor of spring is presented in this attractive dish.

    12 radishes
    12 baby carrots, scrubbed
    1 cup edible pod peas
    1 medium zucchini, cut lengthwise into narrow strips
    8 mushrooms, quartered
    3 tablespoons butter or oil
    1 clove garlic, minced
    ¼ teaspoon thyme
    1 teaspoon parsley
    Salt and freshly ground pepper, to taste

1. In a medium saucepan, steam radishes and carrots in 1 inch of water, about 7 minutes. Drain and set aside.

2. In the same pan steam peas, zucchini and mushrooms in 1 inch of water until tender-crisp, about 4 minutes. Drain and add to radishes and carrots; set aside.

3. In a large skillet, melt butter or oil and sauté garlic; do not burn. Add vegetables, thyme, parsley, salt and pepper. Sauté vegetables until heated through; serve immediately.

4-6 servings

Stir-Fried Vegetables with Black Bean Sauce

This recipe was developed by Yuriko Bullock of Orcas Island. It is an unusual combination of a black bean sauce with vegetables.

 1 carrot, peeled and thinly sliced, diagonally
 2 stalks celery, thinly sliced, diagonally
 6 mushrooms, thinly sliced
 1 small onion, thinly sliced
 2 cups broccoli flowerets
 2 cups cauliflower flowerets
 4 cloves garlic, finely chopped
 BLACK BEAN SAUCE (see below)
 ¼ cup vegetable oil

1. Place prepared vegetables in a large bowl; set aside.
2. Prepare Black Bean Sauce; set aside.
3. In a wok or a large frying pan, heat oil, over high heat. Add vegetables and stir-fry until tender-crisp. When vegetables are cooked, add sauce and cook until thickened and clear; remove from heat. Serve with Honey-Ginger Chicken.

4 servings

BLACK BEAN SAUCE

 1¾ cups water
 3 tablespoons soy sauce
 2½ tablespoons minced dried fermented black beans*
 2 tablespoons cornstarch
 ½ teaspoon salt

In a small bowl combine all ingredients.

*Available in the Oriental section of most supermarkets.

Spinach Pie (Spanakopita)

This traditional Greek dish comes from Orcas Island. The savory filling is highlighted by the delicate phyllo crust.

2 (10-ounce) packages frozen chopped spinach
2 tablespoons olive oil
1 large onion, chopped
4 eggs, beaten
$1/2$ pound feta cheese, crumbled
1 cup small curd cottage cheese
$1/2$ cup finely chopped fresh parsley
2 tablespoons finely chopped mint or 1 teaspoon dried dill weed
1 teaspoon cinnamon
$1/4$ teaspoon nutmeg
$1/4$ teaspoon pepper
$1/2$ pound phyllo pastry sheets, thawed according to package directions
1 cube butter, melted
1 tablespoon sesame seeds

1. In a medium pot, cook spinach according to package directions. Drain in colander and set aside. In the same pot, heat oil over medium heat and sauté onion until soft.

2. In a large bowl, combine eggs. cooked onion, spinach, cheeses, parsley, mint, cinnamon, nutmeg and pepper. Set aside.

3. Preheat oven to 350°. Remove phyllo from package and place on a flat surface; cut sheets in half. Because you will only use one stack, refreeze remaining phyllo. Brush bottom of a 13x9-inch baking dish with melted butter. Remove one sheet of phyllo and place in bottom of baking dish; brush with melted butter. Cover first sheet with second sheet and brush with butter again. Repeat until you have used 10 sheets.

4. Spoon cheese filling evenly over phyllo. Top with remaining 10 phyllo sheets, buttering between each. Cut half-way through phyllo into serving pieces. Pour remaining butter over top; sprinkle with sesame seeds. Bake approximately 1 hour or until pastry is crisp and delicately browned.

18 squares

Swiss Chard Pie

This versatile dish was adapted by Shaw Islander Shirley Baier. Left-over hamburger or pasta can be substituted for the ham and potatoes.

    1/4 cup butter or margarine
    2 medium onions, chopped
    30 leaves swiss chard, torn from stalks and cut into bite-size pieces
    1 cup chopped ham
    1 cup diced cooked potatoes
    2 eggs, slightly beaten
    1/2 cup grated Cheddar cheese
    1/2 cup grated Parmesan cheese
    1 medium tomato, sliced
    1/2 teaspoon dried oregano

1. Preheat oven to 350°. In a large skillet, melt butter and sauté onion until soft. Add chard, tossing quickly to coat with butter; cover with lid to wilt chard. Remove onion and chard mixture from heat and press into a pie pan forming a shell.

2. Sprinkle ham and potatoes over chard; add beaten eggs and Cheddar cheese; blend with a fork. Top with Parmesan cheese and layer with fresh tomato slices; sprinkle with oregano. Bake for 30 minutes.   6 servings

Spinach Stuffed Tomatoes

This colorful dish takes time to prepare but who cares – it's so good!

8 firm ripe tomatoes
1 tablespoon butter or margarine
½ cup finely chopped onion
1 (10-ounce) package frozen spinach, thawed and squeezed dry
⅛ teaspoon nutmeg
½ cup butter or margarine, softened
1 clove garlic, minced
1 tablespoon minced fresh parsley
¼ teaspoon salt
Freshly ground pepper, to taste
½ cup grated Parmesan cheese
¼ cup dry bread crumbs

1. Cut the tops off the tomatoes; remove pulp and seeds, leaving a shell; reserve pulp.

2. In a small frying pan, over medium heat, melt butter and sauté onion until soft. Add reserved tomato pulp, spinach and nutmeg; heat through.

3. Preheat oven to 350°. Fill tomato shells with spinach mixture and place in a greased shallow baking dish.

4. In a small bowl, mix butter, garlic, parsley, salt and pepper. Spread on spinach mixture. In a small bowl, combine Parmesan cheese and bread crumbs and sprinkle on spinach mixture.

5. Bake for 30 minutes or until tomatoes are soft. Brown briefly under the broiler; serve immediately.   8 servings

Stuffed Zucchini

A colorful accompaniment for a barbecued fresh salmon.

3 medium zucchini, ends trimmed
3 tablespoons butter or olive oil
2 tablespoons onion, chopped
2 tablespoons green pepper, chopped fine
¼ cup sliced mushrooms
1 clove garlic, minced
½ cup chopped tomato
¼ cup dry bread crumbs
½ teaspoon dried basil
½ teaspoon salt
⅛ teaspoon freshly ground pepper
⅓ cup Parmesan cheese

1. In a large saucepan, steam whole zucchini in 2 inches of water until tender-crisp, about 10 minutes. Cool and cut in half lengthwise and scoop out centers, leaving about ½-inch thick shell. Place shells in greased baking dish. Chop pulp and reserve in bowl.

2. In a medium frying pan, melt butter and sauté onion, green pepper, mushrooms and garlic, until onion is soft. Add tomatoes and zucchini pulp and continue cooking until tomatoes are soft, about 15 minutes. Add bread crumbs, basil, salt and pepper to mixture.

3. Preheat oven to 350°. Fill zucchini shells with mixture and sprinkle with Parmesan cheese. Bake uncovered for 25-30 minutes and serve immediately.   4-6 servings

Zucchini with Rotini Pasta

A rich cream sauce enhances the flavor of this dish.

12 ounces Rotini spiral pasta
4 tablespoons olive oil
2 tablespoons PESTO SAUCE
   or 1 clove garlic and 1 teaspoon dried basil
5 small zucchini, cut into ¼-inch slices
½ cup sliced mushrooms (optional)
1 cup heavy cream
2 tablespoons chopped fresh parsley
¼ cup Parmesan cheese
Salt and freshly ground pepper, to taste
Parmesan cheese

1. In a large kettle, cook pasta al dente, according to package directions. Drain and return to pot. Add 2 tablespoons olive oil and Pesto Sauce; toss to coat. Cover to keep warm.

2. While pasta is cooking, in a large frying pan, heat 2 tablespoons of oil and sauté garlic and basil (if not using Pesto Sauce). Add zucchini and mushrooms and sauté about 10 minutes.

3. With a slotted spoon, remove zucchini and mushrooms from pan and place in a small bowl; cover to keep warm. Add cream to pan and simmer for 10 minutes or until sauce thickens slightly.

4. Return zucchini and mushrooms to sauce; add parsley, Parmesan, salt and pepper. Add zucchini mixture to pasta and gently toss. Transfer to a warmed serving platter and garnish with additional Parmesan.

8 servings

Zucchini Sautéed with Basil

Use garden-tender zucchini for this easy, yet delectable, dish.

> 2 tablespoons olive oil
> ½ small onion, cut in slices and rings separated
> 6 small zucchini, cut into ¼-inch slices
> 1 cup sliced mushrooms (optional)
> 2 teaspoons fresh or ½ teaspoon dried basil
> Salt and pepper, to taste
> Parmesan cheese

1. In a large frying pan, heat olive oil over medium heat and sauté onion until soft.
2. Add zucchini rounds and mushrooms and sauté until slightly browned; do not overcook. Add basil, salt and pepper. Cover and cook until fork tender. Garnish with Parmesan cheese before serving. 6 servings

Sautéed Crookneck in Cream

A delicate and mild-flavored side dish.

> 4 small crookneck squash, ends trimmed
> 1 ½ tablespoons butter or margarine
> ½ cup light cream
> 2 teaspoons minced fresh parsley
> Salt and freshly ground pepper, to taste

1. Slice crookneck into ¼-inch rounds. In a medium frying pan, over medium-high heat, melt butter and sauté crookneck, about 2-4 minutes; do not overcook.
2. Add cream, cover and simmer over low heat, about 4 minutes. Season with parsley, salt and pepper; serve immediately. 4 servings

Rice Pilaf

A perfect accompaniment for a simple entree.

2 tablespoons butter or margarine
3 green onions (with some tops), thinly sliced
½ cup sliced mushrooms
2 tablespoons slivered almonds (optional)
1½ cups converted rice*
3 cups CHICKEN STOCK
2 tablespoons minced fresh parsley

1. In a medium saucepan, melt butter over medium heat. Sauté onion and mushrooms until soft; add almonds if desired.

2. Add rice and brown slightly. Stir in Chicken Stock and parsley; heat to boiling. Reduce heat to low, cover and simmer until rice is tender, about 20-25 minutes. Toss lightly before serving. 6 servings

*Substitute some wild rice, if desired.

Soups

MATT BROWN

Gillnetter at Mackaye Harbor

Bouillabaisse

The San Juans are famous for a variety of delectable seafoods, making the traditional bouillabaisse a natural choice. We have chosen our favorite seafoods but feel free to make your own choices. Serve with sourdough bread to sop up the delicious sauce.

⅓ cup olive oil
1 onion, chopped
2 cloves garlic, minced
2 ribs celery, chopped
1 green pepper, seeded and chopped
2 cups chopped and peeled tomatoes (about 4 large)
1 (8-ounce) can tomato sauce
6 cups FISH STOCK or CHICKEN STOCK
1 cup dry white wine
¼ cup chopped fresh parsley
1 bay leaf
½ teaspoon crushed fennel seed
¼ teaspoon cayenne
Salt and coarsely ground pepper, to taste
24 mussels, in shells with beards removed
24 steamer clams, in shells
½ pound scallops, without shells
1 pound white fish (cod, snapper or halibut) cut into chunks
1 cup cooked crab meat

1. In a large kettle, heat olive oil over medium heat. Add onion, garlic, celery and green pepper. Sauté until soft, about 5 minutes.

2. Add tomatoes, tomato sauce, stock, wine and all seasonings. Simmer for 30 minutes.

3. Add mussels and steamers. Return to simmer; cook 5 minutes. Add scallops and white fish and cook additional 10 minutes or until shellfish have opened and white fish flakes. Add crab and cook until heated through. Ladle into bowls and serve immediately.   8 servings

Fish Stew

A delicious way to cook the "Catch of the Day." Serve with crusty French bread to enjoy this favorite.

4 slices bacon, diced
⅓ cup olive oil
1 medium onion, chopped
2 cloves garlic, minced
1 green pepper, chopped
1 cup celery with leaves, chopped
1 (16-ounce) can tomatoes, including liquid, chopped
1 (8-ounce) can tomato sauce
2 cups CHICKEN STOCK
½ cup dry white wine
1 bay leaf
½ teaspoon dried oregano
2 tablespoons minced fresh parsley
⅛ teaspoon crushed red pepper
2 pounds skinless white fish fillets (cod, snapper or bass) cut into chunks
Salt and freshly ground pepper, to taste.

1. In a large pot, over medium heat, sauté bacon until crisp. Remove and drain on paper towels; set aside. Discard grease.

2. In the same pot, heat oil and sauté onion, garlic, green pepper and celery until tender. Add next 8 ingredients and reserved bacon. Thin with water, if desired. Simmer for 10 minutes.

3. Add fish, salt and pepper to taste; cook 15 minutes more or until fish flakes when pierced with a fork. Ladle into bowls and serve.

4-6 servings

Old-Fashioned Clam Chowder

Make this classic chowder with tender, sweet butter clams dug at low tide.

4 medium potatoes, diced
2 carrots, sliced
2 celery stalks, chopped
4-6 slices bacon, diced
1 small onion, diced
2 cups chopped clams, drained, reserving liquid
1/4 cup butter or margarine
3 tablespoons flour
1 1/2 cups light cream
1 1/2 cups milk
1/4 teaspoon dried oregano
1/8 dried marjoram
1/4 teaspoon dried thyme
1 tablespoon chopped fresh parsley
Salt and freshly ground pepper, to taste

1. In a large pot, boil potatoes, carrots and celery in enough water to cover. Cook until tender, about 10 minutes; do not drain. Set aside.

2. While vegetables are cooking in a saucepan over medium heat sauté bacon until crisp. Remove bacon and drain on paper towels; set aside. Add onion and cook until soft. Push onion to the side of the pan; add clams and sauté lightly, about 4 minutes. Do not overcook. Remove clams and onion with a slotted spoon and add to vegetables in pot; add reserved bacon.

3. Discard any remaining bacon grease from saucepan. Over medium heat, melt butter and blend in flour. Gradually whisk in cream and milk. Continue cooking, stirring constantly until mixture thickens; do not boil. Add cream sauce, reserved clam liquid and seasonings to cooking pot. Heat through but do not boil. Ladle into bowls and serve.   6 servings

Oyster Stew

This satisfying stew is "first choice" for any oyster lover.

⅓ cup butter or margarine
4 green onions, thinly sliced (without tops)
2 pints shucked oysters, cut in half, reserving liquid
2 tablespoons chopped fresh parsley
½ teaspoon Worcestershire sauce
Dash Tabasco sauce
2 cups light cream
2 cups milk
Salt and freshly ground pepper, to taste
Oyster crackers

1. Melt butter in a 3-quart saucepan. Add onion and sauté until soft, about 3 minutes. Add oysters and parsley; sauté gently until edges start to curl, about 3 or 4 minutes. Do not overcook, or oysters will become tough.

2. Add remaining ingredients, including reserved oyster liquid. Heat through, over medium-high, stirring occasionally; do not boil. Ladle into bowls and serve with oyster crackers or crusty French bread.

4 servings

Creamy Seafood Bisque

This elegant soup is a rich combination of seafood in a creamy broth.

6 tablespoons butter or margarine
1 medium onion, chopped
1 cup chopped celery, with leaves
5 tablespoons flour
2 cups CHICKEN STOCK
3 cups light cream
½ cup dry white wine or vermouth
1 tablespoon chopped fresh parsley
Dash Tabasco sauce
1 teaspoon paprika
1 teaspoon salt
¼ teaspoon white pepper
1 pound cooked seafood (crab meat, scallops or shrimp)

Breads

PETER CAPEN   *San Juan Island Barn*

1. In a large pot, melt butter over medium heat. Sauté onion and celery until tender. Blend in flour and gradually whisk in Chicken Stock, cream and wine. Stir constantly until soup thickens; do not boil. Season with parsley, Tabasco sauce, and paprika; salt and pepper to taste.

2. Gently fold in seafood and heat through over low heat. Serve immediately.   6 servings

Cream of Shaggy Mane Soup

Look for Shaggy Manes in autumn along gravelly roads or paths the day after a rain. Other mushrooms may be substituted but Shaggies have their own special flavor. Use them immediately after picking as they quickly begin to "ink."

1/3 cup butter or margarine
4 cups sliced raw Shaggy Manes, cleaned
1/4 cup flour
3 cups CHICKEN STOCK
4 cups light cream
1/2 cup grated Cheddar cheese
Salt and freshly ground pepper, to taste

1. In a medium pot, melt butter and sauté mushrooms until tender, about 15 minutes. Remove mushrooms and set aside.

2. Blend in flour and gradually whisk in Chicken Stock and cream. Stir constantly until soup thickens; do not boil. Return mushrooms to stock and heat through.

3. Stir in cheese and allow to melt. Salt and pepper to taste. Serve immediately.   4-6 servings

Curried Broccoli Soup

Curry adds a lively flavor to this tasty soup.

    2 pounds broccoli, stems peeled and sliced, tops broken into flowerets
    1 stalk celery, chopped
    ¼ cup butter or margarine
    1 onion, chopped
    1 clove garlic, minced
    ⅓ cup flour
    2 teaspoons curry powder
    4 cups CHICKEN STOCK
    3 cups light cream
    Salt and freshly ground pepper, to taste

1. In a large pot, steam broccoli and celery until tender. Drain, discarding water. Set aside 1 cup of flowerets. Purée remaining broccoli and celery in food processor or blender; set aside.

2. In a large pot, melt butter, sauté onion and garlic until soft. Blend in flour and curry. Gradually whisk in Chicken Stock and cream. Stir constantly until soup thickens; do not boil. Add all the broccoli and heat through. Season to taste with salt and pepper.   8 servings

Cheddar Cheese Soup

The creamy broth is delicately flavored with cheese.

2 cups CHICKEN STOCK
3 medium carrots, thinly sliced
2 celery stalks, thinly sliced
2 tablespoons butter or margarine
2 tablespoons minced onion
⅓ cup flour
2 cups grated Cheddar cheese
4 cups milk
¼ teaspoon Tabasco sauce
Salt and freshly ground pepper, to taste

1. In a medium saucepan, bring Chicken Stock to a boil; add carrots and celery. Reduce heat and simmer about 15 minutes or until vegetables are tender. Set aside; do not drain.

2. In a large pot, melt butter and sauté onion until soft. Blend in flour and gradually whisk in reserved Chicken Stock and vegetables. Bring to a boil, stirring until soup thickens slightly.

3. Add cheese and allow to melt. Whisk in milk; heat through but do not boil. Season with Tabasco sauce, salt and pepper. 6 servings

Cream of Spinach Soup

The New Bay Cafe on Lopez Island offers delicious homecooked food from country-style breakfasts to Mexican specialties. This hearty and nutritious soup is a favorite of their customers.

2 medium carrots, chopped
2 medium onions, chopped
2 cloves garlic, minced
2 medium potatoes, diced
2 pounds spinach, cleaned
⅔ cup butter or margarine
⅔ cup flour
4 cups milk
2 teaspoons dried basil
½ teaspoon dried thyme
Salt and freshly ground pepper, to taste
Sour cream

1. In a large pot, combine first 4 ingredients; add enough water to cover and cook until tender. Put water and vegetables in blender or food processor and purée; set aside.

2. In same pot, steam spinach in 2 cups of water and purée. Return to same pot; set aside.

3. In a medium saucepan, melt butter and blend in flour. Gradually whisk in milk. Continue cooking, stirring constantly until sauce is thick and smooth.

4. Add vegetable purée to spinach in large pot; mix thoroughly. Add white sauce and season with basil, thyme, salt and pepper. Heat through; do not boil.

5. Ladle into serving bowls and top with a dollop of sour cream.

8 servings

Black Bean Soup

This hearty soup is warming on a blustery Northwest day. The black beans cook to a deep purple-brown.

2½ cups black beans (1 pound), washed and soaked overnight in 8 cups cold water
¼ cup olive or vegetable oil
2 cloves garlic, minced
1 large onion, chopped
2 stalks celery, chopped including leaves
1 medium carrot, peeled and chopped
6 cups CHICKEN or BEEF STOCK or water
1 ham bone or ham hock
2 tomatoes, peeled and seeded, coarsely chopped
2 tablespoons chopped parsley
½ teaspoon dried thyme
1 tablespoon ground cumin
½ teaspoon red pepper flakes
1 bay leaf
½ teaspoon salt
⅛ teaspoon freshly ground pepper
¼ cup dry sherry (optional)
1 lemon, sliced
Sour cream or yogurt

1. In a large pot, heat oil over medium heat. Sauté garlic, onion, celery, and carrot until onion is soft, about 8 minutes.

2. Drain and rinse beans. Place in cooking pot with sautéed vegetables. Add stock or water and next 9 ingredients. Bring to a boil; reduce heat and cover. Simmer 4 hours or until beans are tender. Add more broth or water if soup seems too thick.

3. Remove ham bone and pull off any meat; return to pot.

4. Add sherry and additional seasonings to taste; heat through. Serve with a lemon slice and sour cream or yogurt as garnish.   8 servings

Fidalgo Lentil Soup

Ken Jacot of Fidalgo Island provided us with this delicious soup recipe. The robust flavor appeals to the hearty appetite.

1 pound lentils, rinsed and soaked overnight in 8 cups cold water
¼ pound slab bacon, coarsely chopped
2 tablespoons vegetable oil
1 onion, chopped
2 stalks celery, sliced
2 carrots, peeled and diced
2 cloves garlic, minced
8 cups CHICKEN or BEEF STOCK
1 (16-ounce) can tomatoes, coarsely chopped
1 (15-ounce) package smoked sausage links, cut in half
2 tablespoons burgandy wine
2 tablespoons brown sugar
1 tablespoon cider vinegar
2 bay leaves
1 teaspoon dried thyme
Salt and freshly ground pepper, to taste
Parmesan cheese

1. In a large pot, over medium heat, fry bacon until crisp. Remove bacon and drain; set aside. Discard grease. Drain and rinse lentils.

2. In the same pot, heat oil. Sauté onion, celery, carrots, and garlic until tender. Add stock, lentils, tomatoes, sausages, wine, sugar, vinegar, bay leaves and reserved bacon. Heat soup to boiling. Skim off foam if necessary.

3. Reduce heat; add thyme, salt and pepper to taste. Cover and simmer about 2 hours or until soup is of desired thickness. Ladle into bowls, garnish with Parmesan and serve.   6 servings

Gazpacho

A refreshing cold soup that is ideal for a summer luncheon.

3 cups diced fresh tomatoes, peeled or 1 (1¾-pound) can diced tomatoes,
   undrained
6 green onions, chopped
1 stalk celery, finely sliced
1 cucumber, peeled and coarsely chopped
1 clove garlic, minced
1 tablespoon chopped fresh parsley or cilantro
2 cups tomato juice or vegetable juice
2 tablespoons red wine vinegar
2 tablespoons fresh lemon juice
Dash of Tabasco sauce
½ teaspoon dried basil
Parsley

1. In a large bowl, combine all ingredients. Gazpacho can be puréed in a food processor or blender, if desired. Cover and chill for at least 2 hours.

2. Serve in chilled bowls and garnish with parsley.   4-6 servings

Meatball Soup

Corn "masa" adds flavor to the meatballs in this traditional Spanish soup. Yadira Young of Guemes Island shared her mother's favorite recipe with us. Let the bounty of your harvest determine the vegetables you choose.

1 pound ground beef
1/2 cup prepared corn "masa"* or dry bread crumbs
2 cloves garlic, minced
1/4 cup finely chopped onion
1/2 green bell pepper, finely chopped
2 tablespoons minced parsley
3/4 teaspoon salt
1/4 teaspoon pepper
5 cups BEEF STOCK
2 potatoes, peeled and cut into 1/2-inch cubes
2 cups sliced carrots
1 cup sliced celery
1/4 cup chopped green bell pepper
1 tablespoon diced onion
1 clove garlic, minced
1 teaspoon dried thyme
1 teaspoon salt
1/2 teaspoon pepper
1 zucchini, cut into chunks

1. In a medium bowl, combine beef, corn masa, garlic, onion, green pepper, parsley, salt and pepper. Shape into tiny, 1-inch, meatballs. Cover bowl and set aside.

2. In a large kettle, combine remaining ingredients, except zucchini. Bring to a boil and reduce heat to simmer for 5 minutes. Add zucchini and return pot to a rolling boil. Soup must be boiling when meatballs are added or they will disintegrate. Add meatballs and continue to boil 5-7 minutes; reduce heat and simmer 15 minutes more. Ladle into serving bowls.

6 servings

*Corn "masa" is available in the foreign food section at the supermarket.

French Onion Soup

This traditional French soup, topped with toast and melted cheese, is a favorite among San Juan Islanders.

2 tablespoons butter or margarine
2 tablespoons olive oil
6 large yellow onions, thinly sliced
8 cups BEEF STOCK
1/3 cup dry red wine (optional)
1 bay leaf
1/4 teaspoon freshly ground pepper
8 slices day old French bread, sliced 1/2-inch thick
1/3 cup butter or margarine
2 cups mixed grated Gruyére and Parmesan cheese

1. In a large pot, over medium heat, melt butter and oil. Add onion and sauté about 5 minutes. Cover and continue cooking until soft.

2. Stir in Beef Stock and wine. Season with bay leaf and pepper.

3. Bring soup to a boil. Reduce heat and simmer for 45 minutes, uncovered. Skim surface as needed.

4. While soup is simmering, place sliced French bread on baking sheet. Bake in 300° oven for 20-25 minutes or until lightly toasted; butter toast and set aside.

5. Ladle soup into oven-proof soup bowls. Top with a slice of toasted French bread and sprinkle with cheeses. Broil quickly until cheese bubbles and is lightly toasted. Serve immediately.   8 servings

Homemade Stocks

Use these flavorful stocks for soups, sauces and stews. Prepare them on a rainy day and freeze for a later use.

CHICKEN STOCK

1 large chicken (about 3 pounds)
3 quarts cold water
1 large onion, quartered
2 cloves garlic
2 stalks celery with leaves, cut in half
2 carrots, peeled and cut in half
½ teaspoon dried basil
½ teaspoon dried thyme
1 tablespoon minced fresh parsley
1 bay leaf
1 teaspoon salt
6 peppercorns

1. In a large stock pot, combine all ingredients. Bring slowly to a boil. Skim off the fat and froth as necessary. Simmer, partially covered, for 2 hours or until meat can be pulled from the bones. Save meat for another use.

2. Strain the stock through a sieve into a large container. Cover and refrigerate or divide into airtight containers and freeze for later use.

2½ quarts

BEEF STOCK

3 tablespoons olive oil
2 onions, chopped
2 carrots, peeled and cut in half
2 stalks celery with leaves, cut in half
2 leeks, chopped (optional)
1 1/2 pounds lean beef
1 1/2 pounds beef bones
2 cloves garlic
3 quarts water
1/2 teaspoon dried thyme
8 sprigs parsley
1 bay leaf
1 teaspoon salt
6 peppercorns

1. In a large stock pot, over medium heat, heat oil and sauté onion, carrots, celery and leeks until tender. Add remaining ingredients; bring to a boil and skim off the fat and froth from the surface, as necessary. Simmer partially covered for 2-3 hours.

2. Remove the beef and bones; save beef for another use. Strain the stock through a sieve into a large container. Allow to cool; skim off any remaining fat.

3. Cover and refrigerate stock or divide into airtight containers and freeze for later use.   2 quarts

FISH STOCK

This is a savory stock to use for poaching fish or as a base for chowders, fish stews and sauces.

    2 pounds white fish (trimmings, bones and heads, but no gills)
      rinsed thoroughly and blood removed
    1 onion, quartered
    1 stalk celery, sliced and cut in half
    4 sprigs parsley
    1 tablespoon lemon juice
    1 cup dry white wine
    4 cups water
    1 bay leaf
    1 teaspoon dried thyme
    1 teaspoon salt
    6 peppercorns

1. In a large pot, combine all ingredients. Bring to a boil; reduce heat and simmer for 30 minutes; skim off any froth.

2. Strain stock through a sieve into a large container. Cover and refrigerate or divide into airtight container and freeze for later use.   1 quart

Lemon Poppy Seed Bread

Fresh lemon gives this moist bread a luscious flavor.

    6 tablespoons butter or margarine
    1 cup sugar
    2 eggs
    1 teaspoon dried lemon rind or grated rind of 1 lemon
    1 1/2 cups flour
    1 1/2 teaspoons baking powder
    1/2 teaspoon salt
    1/2 cup milk
    1/3 cup poppy seeds
    1/2 cup chopped nuts
    LEMON GLAZE (see below)

1. Preheat oven to 350°. In a large bowl, beat together butter and sugar until well blended. Add eggs, one at a time, beating well after each addition.

2. To butter mixture, add lemon rind, flour, baking powder and salt, alternating with milk. Stir in poppy seeds and nuts. Turn batter into greased loaf pan. Bake for 50 minutes or until toothpick inserted in center of bread comes out clean.

3. While bread is baking, prepare Lemon Glaze. Remove bread from oven; make holes in top of warm bread with fork tines. Pour glaze over loaf and let cool in pan on wire rack. Remove from pan and slice.   1 loaf

LEMON GLAZE

    Juice of 1 lemon
    1/4 cup sugar

In a small saucepan, heat lemon juice and sugar. Simmer gently for 5 minutes, stirring occasionally.

Berry Muffins

Make these sweet muffins when blueberries and raspberries are ripe in July and August.

BLUEBERRY MUFFINS

> 1/4 cup butter or margarine, at room temperature
> 2 eggs
> 3/4 cup sugar
> 1/2 teaspoon salt
> 1/2 cup milk
> 1 teaspoon vanilla
> 2 cups all-purpose flour
> 2 teaspoons baking powder
> 2 cups fresh or frozen blueberries

1. Preheat oven to 350°. In a large bowl, beat butter, eggs, sugar and salt until well blended. Stir in milk and vanilla; set aside.

2. In a large bowl, sift flour with baking powder. Pour egg mixture over flour and baking powder and stir to blend.

3. Gently fold blueberries into batter. Fill greased muffin cups two-thirds full with batter. Bake for 25 minutes. Remove from oven and immediately turn out onto a wire rack. 1 dozen

RASPBERRY MUFFINS

> 1/4 cup butter or margarine, at room temperature
> 1 large egg
> 1/4 cup packed brown sugar
> 1/4 cup granulated sugar
> 1/2 teaspoon salt
> 3/4 cup buttermilk
> 2 cups all-purpose flour
> 1/2 teaspoon baking soda
> 1 teaspoon ground cinnamon
> 1 teaspoon grated lemon peel
> 1 cup fresh raspberries

1. Preheat oven to 375°. In a large bowl, beat butter, egg, sugars and salt until well blended. Stir in buttermilk; set aside.

2. In a large bowl, sift together flour, baking soda and cinnamon. Pour egg mixture over dry ingredients and stir to blend; add lemon peel.

3. Gently fold raspberries into batter. Fill greased muffin cups two-thirds full with batter. Bake for 25 minutes. Remove from oven and immediately turn out onto a wire rack.   1 dozen

Captain's Crunch

This is an easy way to prepare a fresh coffee cake on your boat while cruising the San Juans. It's a favorite at the Wharfside Bed and Breakfast in Friday Harbor on San Juan Island.

    2 tablespoons butter or margarine, at room temperature
    2 baking apples, peeled and chopped
    1 (8-ounce) can Pillsbury Butterflake Dinner Rolls
    1 egg, lightly beaten
    1/3 cup firmly packed brown sugar
    1/3 cup light corn syrup
    1/4 teaspoon cinnamon
    Dash nutmeg
    1 1/2 teaspoons sherry or vanilla
    2/3 cup chopped walnuts, pecans or almonds
    Glaze (optional)
    1/3 cup powdered sugar
    1/4 teaspoon vanilla
    1-2 teaspoons milk

1. Preheat oven to 350°. Grease the bottom of a 9-inch round cake pan with 1 tablespoon butter. Spread three-fourths of the apples into the greased cake pan.

2. Separate dough into 12 biscuits, cut each into four pieces. Arrange pieces point-side up over apples. Top with remaining apples.

3. In a small bowl, combine next 7 ingredients and spoon over apples. Bake for 30 to 35 minutes, or until apples are golden brown. Cool for 5 minutes and remove from pan. Serve with cream, if desired.

4. To make glaze, blend glaze ingredients and drizzle over warm cake. Serve warm.   6-8 servings

Crusty French Bread

French bread is easy-to-make and can add the crowning touch to any meal.

2½ teaspoons dry yeast (1 package)
1¼ cups warm water (110°)
1 tablespoon sugar
1½ teaspoons salt
3 cups flour*
2 teaspoons cornmeal

1. In a large mixing bowl, dissolve yeast in warm water. Stir in sugar, salt and 2 cups flour; mix thoroughly. Gradually add remaining flour until dough begins to form a ball and pull away from the side of the bowl.

2. Knead on a lightly floured surface for 5-8 minutes or until dough is smooth and elastic. Put dough in a greased bowl; turn over to grease top of dough. Cover bowl with clear plastic or a damp towel. Let rise in a warm place (about 80°) until double, about 1 hour.

3. Lightly grease baking sheet or French bread pan and sprinkle with cornmeal. Punch down dough and place on lightly floured board; knead to squeeze out air bubbles. Shape dough into an oblong loaf. With a sharp knife, make three diagonal cuts in top of loaf; place on prepared pan. Let dough rise, uncovered, until double, about 45 minutes. Before baking, brush top of loaf with 2 teaspoons of water for a crispy crust. Or, for a shiny crust, combine egg white and 2 teaspoons of water and brush top of loaf.

4. While bread is rising, preheat oven to 400°. To ensure a crisp crust, spray oven walls with water or place a shallow pan of hot water in bottom of oven while baking bread. Bake for 35-40 minutes, or until golden brown. Remove from pan; place on wire rack to cool.   1 loaf

*Substitute part of the white flour with whole wheat flour, if desired.

Breadsticks

Breadsticks add a festive touch to any meal.

2½ teaspoons dry yeast (1 package)
⅔ cup warm water (110°)
1 tablespoon sugar
1 teaspoon salt
¼ cup olive or vegetable oil
2-2¼ cups all purpose flour
2 tablespoons vegetable oil
1 egg white
1 tablespoon water
½ cup toasted sesame seeds (optional)

1. In a large mixing bowl, dissolve yeast in warm water. Stir in sugar, salt and oil. Slowly add 1 cup flour, beating until smooth. Gradually add remaining flour until dough begins to form a ball and pull away from side of the bowl.

2. Knead on a lightly floured surface for 5-8 minutes or until dough is smooth and elastic. Shape dough into a long roll, about 12 inches. With a sharp knife, cut into 36 equal parts. Roll each part into a 10-inch rope. Arrange about 1 inch apart on oiled baking sheets. (Freeze at this point if desired. Cover baking sheet with plastic wrap and place in freezer. Transfer frozen breadsticks to plastic bags and store up to four weeks. To bake, arrange on ungreased baking sheet, cover and allow to thaw for 15 minutes.)

3. Preheat oven to 325°. Cover thawed or unfrozen breadsticks with plastic wrap or damp cloth and allow to rise in a warm place until puffy, about 15 to 20 minutes.

4. In a small bowl, beat egg white and water with a fork and brush each breadstick lightly. Sprinkle with sesame seeds, if desired. Bake for 20 to 25 minutes or until golden brown. Remove from pan; place on wire rack to cool. Serve with butter.   1½ dozen breadsticks

Focaccia

Jane Nelson brought this savory flat-bread recipe back from Italy. It's one of Shaw Island's favorites.

2½ teaspoons dry yeast (1 package)
1½ cups warm water (110°)
1 teaspoon salt
2 cups unbleached white flour
1-1½ cups whole wheat flour
¼ cup olive oil
½ tomato, coarsely chopped and drained
½ cup seeded and sliced Greek olives
1 (6-ounce) jar marinated artichoke hearts, drained and sliced
½ cup chopped onion
1½ tablespoons grated Parmesan cheese
1 teaspoon dried or fresh rosemary sprigs or oregano

1. In a large mixing bowl, dissolve yeast in warm water; stir in salt. Slowly add 1 cup flour and stir until thoroughly mixed. Gradually add remaining unbleached flour and enough whole wheat flour until dough begins to form a ball and pulls away from side of bowl.

2. Knead on a lightly floured board until dough is smooth and elastic. Place dough in a bowl rinsed with hot water. Cover bowl and let rise in a warm place (about 80°) until double, about 40 minutes.

3. Generously grease a 10x15-inch jelly-roll pan with 2 tablespoons olive oil. Punch down dough and roll out about ½-inch thick. Transfer dough to pan and pat out to pan edges.

4. Preheat oven to 400°. Using fingers, firmly press toppings into dough. Brush with remaining olive oil and sprinkle with Parmesan and herb. Raise again, about 15 minutes. Bake in lower third of oven for 20-25 minutes or until edges of crust are well browned. Cut into 4-inch squares; serve hot and watch it disappear!

8-10 servings

Lopez Whole Wheat Bread

Raisins, dried fruits and nuts can be added to this wholesome bread. It is an unusual yeast bread because it only rises once. It is popular at Holly B's Bakery on Lopez Island.

3 cups warm water (110°)
²/₃ cup honey
3¹/₃ tablespoons dry yeast (4 packages)
¹/₂ cup sesame seeds or sunflower seeds or a combination
2 teaspoons salt
2 cups wheat germ
4 cups whole wheat flour

1. In a large mixing bowl, mix water and honey together. Sprinkle in yeast and allow bubbles to form. Stir in remaining ingredients.

2. Pour batter into 2 greased 9x5-inch loaf pans. Place in a warm place and let rise until the dough nearly reaches the top. Bake at 350° for 45 minutes or until golden. Remove bread from pans and cool on a wire rack. Loaves will be heavier than most breads.

2 loaves

Aunt Chris' Panetone

Dawn's aunt makes this traditional Italian bread every Christmas, and her family always looks forward to a package. They enjoy it toasted with butter.

1/2 cup sugar
2 cups warm water (110°)
2 1/2 tablespoons dry yeast (3 packages)
1 quart scalded milk
1/2 cup butter
1 cup orange juice
1 teaspoon lemon extract
1 teaspoon vanilla extract
1 teaspoon nutmeg
1 tablespoon anise seed, soaked in 2 tablespoons warm water
3 eggs, beaten
12 cups flour
1 1/2 cups sugar
1 tablespoon salt
8 ounces citron
4 ounces candied orange peel
4 ounces candied lemon peel
16 ounces light raisins
16 ounces dark raisins
1 cup chopped almonds
1 1/2 cups pine nuts
1/3 cup melted butter

1. In a medium bowl, dissolve 1/2 cup sugar in 2 cups warm water. Sprinkle yeast over water and stir with a wooden spoon until dissolved; set aside.

2. In a medium saucepan, scald milk, remove from heat and add butter. After butter has melted, add orange juice, lemon extract, vanilla, nutmeg, anise seeds and soaking water. Cool to lukewarm and add beaten eggs. Stir in reserved yeast mixture; set aside.

3. In a large mixing bowl, combine flour, 1 1/2 cups sugar, salt, candied fruits, raisins and nuts; stir to blend. Make a hole in the mixture and pour in half of the milk mixture; mix thoroughly. Gradually add the remaining milk mixture as needed to make a smooth dough. When dough is stiff enough to handle, knead on a floured board until dough is smooth and elastic.

4. Place dough in two greased bowls, turn over to grease tops of dough. Cover bowls with clear plastic wrap or damp cloth. Let rise until doubled, about two hours.

5. Punch down dough and place on lightly floured board. Divide dough into fourths and knead each loaf until smooth. Place each loaf into a greased bread pan. Brush tops with melted butter; cover and let rise until doubled. (It may take as long as 2 hours.) Keep in a warm place at all times.

6. While bread is rising, preheat oven to 350°. Bake for 45 minutes or until golden brown. Remove from pans; place on wire racks to cool.

4 loaves

Cinnamon Bread

This delicious bread is served at the Tucker and Blair Houses, located at Friday Harbor on San Juan Island. These bed and breakfast inns provide a congenial and comfortable atmosphere.

2½ teaspoons dry yeast (1 package)
¼ cup warm water (110°)
⅔ cup milk (110°)
1 teaspoon salt
½ cup butter, melted and cooled
½ cup granulated sugar
2 eggs, beaten
3 to 3½ cups all-purpose flour
1½ teaspoons ground cinnamon
½ cup powdered sugar, unsifted
½ teaspoon vanilla extract
1 tablespoon milk

1. In a mixing bowl, combine yeast and water; let stand until bubbly. Stir in milk, salt and ¼ cup butter and ¼ cup sugar. Add eggs and 1½ cups of flour, beat until smooth. Add remaining flour until dough begins to form a ball and pull away from side of bowl.

2. Put dough in greased bowl and turn over to grease top of dough. Cover and let rise in a warm place until doubled, about 1 hour. Turn dough onto a lightly floured board and knead lightly, about 5 minutes, adding more flour as needed.

3. Roll out into a 9x18-inch rectangle. Brush with 2 tablespoons of the remaining butter. Mix the remaining ¼ cup granulated sugar with cinnamon; sprinkle over dough.

4. Roll up tightly, like a jelly roll. Turn loaf over and pinch a seam down the center. Put shaped loaf seam side down into a greased 9x5-inch loaf pan. Brush top with remaining 2 tablespoons butter. Cover and let rise until almost doubled, about 45 minutes.

5. Bake in a 350° oven, about 30-35 minutes, or until loaf is nicely browned and sounds hollow when tapped. Turn loaf out of pan onto a rack. Stir together powdered sugar, vanilla and 1 tablespoon milk. While bread is still warm, drizzle glaze over top and let it run down the sides. Cool before slicing or wrapping.   1 loaf

Granola

Begin your morning with this healthful cereal.

5 cups regular rolled oats
1 cup wheat flakes (optional)
¾ cup raw sunflower seeds
2 cups large flaked coconut*
¼ cup wheat germ
1 cup unsalted cashews or peanuts
½ cup vegetable oil
½ cup honey
1 teaspoon vanilla
1 cup raisins (optional)

1. Preheat oven to 325°. In a large bowl, combine first 6 ingredients and set aside.

2. In a small saucepan, over medium-low, heat oil and honey; do not boil. Remove from heat and add vanilla. Pour warm honey mixture over dry ingredients; stir to coat.

3. Grease a 13x9-inch baking pan. Pour granola into pan and bake for 20 minutes or until toasted, stirring occasionally.

4. Remove from oven and cool, stirring frequently to prevent sticking. Add raisins, if desired. Store in air-tight containers. Serve with milk, yogurt or fruit.   2½ quarts

*Available in health food stores

Gramma's Raisin Bread

At ninety-five, Guemes Island's Gramma Veal was still delighting her guests with a gift of her special bread. It is delicious toasted.

1 (15-ounce) box raisins (2½ cups)
1 cup boiling water
1½ cups milk
½ cup sugar
2 teaspoons salt
½ cup margarine
1 egg, beaten
1½ tablespoons dry yeast (2 packages)
½ cup warm water (110°)
6 cups all-purpose flour
½ cup sugar
1 tablespoon ground cinnamon
2 tablespoons butter or margarine

1. To plump raisins, place in a bowl with the boiling water; set aside. In a small saucepan, scald milk by bringing it to a low simmer.

2. Pour heated milk into a large mixing bowl; add sugar, salt and margarine and stir until margarine is melted. Cook to lukewarm and add beaten egg. Dissolve yeast in the ½ cup warm water; add to milk mixture.

3. Drain raisins and discard water; pat dry with paper towel. Add raisins to milk mixture.

4. Slowly add 1 cup flour to milk mixture, beating until smooth. Gradually add remaining flour until dough begins to form a ball and pull away from side of the bowl.

5. Knead on a lightly floured surface for 5-8 minutes or until dough is smooth and elastic. Put dough in a greased bowl, turn over to grease top of dough. Cover bowl with clear plastic or a damp towel. Let rise in a warm place (about 80°) until double, about 1½ hours.

6. Punch down dough and place on a lightly floured board. Divide dough into thirds and roll into balls. Using a rolling pin, roll each ball into a 9-inch diameter circle. Sprinkle each circle with sugar and cinnamon. Roll dough up like a jelly roll and place, seam side down, into greased bread pans. Cover pans with clear plastic or a damp towel. Let rise in a warm place (about 80°) until double, about 1 hour.

7. While bread is rising, preheat oven to 350°. Bake for 45 minutes or until bread sounds hollow when tapped. If bread browns too quickly, cover with foil. Remove from pans; place on wire rack to cool. Rub top crust with butter, if a soft crust is desired.   3 loaves

Rice Buttermilk Pancakes

These pancakes are always a favorite at Janice's house.

BLUEBERRY SYRUP (optional – see page 191)
2 eggs
2 cups buttermilk
1/4 cup vegetable oil
2 cups all-purpose flour*
3/4 teaspoon baking powder
1 1/4 teaspoons baking soda
Dash salt
1/2 cup cooked rice
1/4 cup margarine

1. Prepare Blueberry Syrup, if desired.
2. In a mixing bowl beat eggs, add buttermilk and oil. Beat in remaining 4 ingredients; stir in rice.
3. Grease a hot griddle with 1 tablespoon margarine and pour batter from large spoon onto hot griddle. When they are nicely browned and top is full of unbroken bubbles, turn pancakes and cook other side until golden brown. Repeat, using remaining batter. Serve warm with syrup.

                                                              4 servings

*Or substitute part white flour for whole wheat flour, wheat germ or bran.

Rose Hip Syrup

Collecting autumn rose hips may become a tradition in your family after you try Rose Hip Syrup. Harvest rose hips in October when they are bright red.

1 quart ripe rose hips, sorted, stemmed and washed
2 cups fresh orange juice
4 cups sugar
1/2 package powdered pectin
2 teaspoons zested orange rind
Red food coloring (optional)

1. To prepare juice: Grind rose hips in a food processor or meat grinder. Transfer pulp to a large kettle with enough orange juice to cover. Bring to a boil, reduce heat and simmer for 15 minutes. Place cooked fruit and liquid in a jelly bag, or cheese cloth and a colander and allow juices to drain into a large pot. Do not squeeze bag, or syrup will be cloudy.

2. Juice should measure 4 cups. If not, add enough strained orange juice to measure 4 cups. Pour into a large pot, add sugar and pectin. Use a zester to make orange rind curls and add to syrup.

3. Bring to a rolling boil and boil 2 minutes stirring constantly. Remove from heat and skim off foam. Add food coloring, if desired. Pour hot syrup into sterile canning jars to within 1/2-inch of top. Seal with sterile canning lids and process in boiling water bath for 10 minutes.

4. Remove from canner and let cool. Store in a cool, dark room.

4 cups

Blueberry Syrup

1 tablespoon cornstarch
2 teaspoons lemon juice
1/2 cup sugar
1/2 cup water
1 (12-ounce) package frozen blueberries

In a saucepan, mix cornstarch, lemon juice, sugar and water. Add frozen blueberries. Cover pan and cook over medium heat to thicken, stirring occasionally.

2 cups

Cleo's Waffles

These delicious waffles can become a Sunday morning habit.

4 eggs, separated
1/3 cup vegetable oil
1 3/4 cups buttermilk
1 1/2 cups all-purpose flour*
2 teaspoons baking powder
1 teaspoon baking soda
Dash salt
Margarine
Syrup

1. Preheat waffle iron. In a large mixing bowl, beat egg whites until stiff. Remove from bowl and set aside.

2. Place egg yolks in mixing bowl and beat until frothy. Add oil and buttermilk; mix thoroughly.

3. Add flour, baking powder, soda and salt to egg yolk mixture; mix well. Fold in reserved egg whites.

4. Grease waffle iron with margarine and ladle batter onto hot iron. Cook until golden. Serve with syrup or desired topping.

4 servings.

*Or substitute part of the white flour with whole wheat flour.

Flatbread

Serve this traditional crispy flatbread with butter or enjoy with a spread such as our Eggplant Pâté.

½ tablespoon sugar
1¼ teaspoons dry yeast (½ package)
1 cup warm water (110°)
2¼-2½ cups unbleached white flour*
¼ cup (4 tablespoons) butter, melted and cooled
2 teaspoons salt

1. In a large mixing bowl, dissolve sugar and yeast in warm water. Stir in 1 cup flour and mix thoroughly. Gradually add remaining flour until dough begins to form a ball and pull away from the side of the bowl. Cover and let rest for 15 minutes.

2. Knead dough on a lightly floured surface for 5-8 minutes or until it becomes smooth and elastic. Put dough in a greased bowl, turn over to grease top of dough; cover with clear plastic and let rise in a warm place (about 80°) until doubled, 1-1½ hours.

3. Preheat oven to 375°. Lightly grease 2 large baking sheets and sprinkle with corn meal. Divide dough into 4 equal pieces and roll into balls. Roll each ball into a 12-inch circle and place on baking sheets. Bake 10 to 12 minutes or until bottom begins to brown. Bread should be crisp and bubbly. Remove from pan and cool on wire racks.   4 servings

*Or substitute part of the white flour with whole wheat flour.

Desserts

MATT BROWN   *Islands Sunset*

Apple-Cranberry Pie

Sarah Spaeth of Lopez Island created this pie with a rich shortbread crust. It makes an ideal holiday dessert.

Crust
3 cups flour
1 1/2 cups cold butter (3 cubes)
1 egg, lightly beaten
1 tablespoon cider vinegar or lemon juice
1/2 teaspoon salt
Water
Filling
3 cups chopped apples, peel if desired
1 cup whole cranberries
1 cup sour cream
1 egg
3/4 cup sugar
3 tablespoons flour
1/2 teaspoon lemon or orange rind
1/2 teaspoon vanilla
Topping
1/4 cup flour
1/2 cup sugar
1 teaspoon cinnamon
6 tablespoons butter or margarine

1. To prepare crust: In a large bowl, combine flour and butter with a pastry blender or fork until butter is the size of peas. Add egg, vinegar, salt and enough water until mixture is evenly moistened. Form into two balls, reserving one for another use; you may freeze if desired. Transfer ball to a lightly floured board and roll out to fit into a 10-inch pie pan. Place in pie pan, trim and crimp edges.

2. To prepare filling: Preheat oven to 375°. In a large bowl, combine all filling ingredients. Pour into pie crust. Bake 30 minutes.

3. To prepare topping: Combine flour, sugar and cinnamon. Cut in butter with a pastry blender or fork to make a crumbly topping. Sprinkle on baked pie and bake an additional 15 minutes or until top is golden brown.

10-inch pie

Sour-Cream Apple Pie

The nutty crunch of the topping sets off the creamy apple filling.

Crust
1¾ cups all-purpose flour
2 tablespoons sugar
½ teaspoon cinnamon
½ teaspoon salt
10 tablespoons butter or margarine
¼ cup water or apple cider, chilled
Filling
1 cup sour cream
¾ cup sugar
3 tablespoons flour
1 egg, lightly beaten
1½ teaspoons vanilla
¼ teaspoon salt
6 baking apples (Golden Delicious, Granny Smith or Jonathan) (4 cups) peeled,
   cored and sliced
⅓ cup raisins (optional)
Topping
½ cup chopped walnuts
⅓ cup brown sugar
⅓ cup flour
1 teaspoon cinnamon
⅓ cup butter or margarine

1. To prepare crust: In a mixing bowl, combine flour, sugar, cinnamon and salt. With a pastry blender or a fork, cut in butter until mixture resembles coarse meal. Add liquid and toss until mixture is evenly moistened. Form into a ball and transfer to a lightly floured board. Roll out to fit into a 10-inch pie pan. Place in pan; trim and crimp edges.

2. To prepare filling: Preheat oven to 450°. In a large bowl, combine sour cream, sugar, flour, egg, vanilla and salt; mix well. Add apples and raisins and toss to coat. Pour apple filling in pie crust. Bake for 10 minutes. Reduce temperature to 350° and continue baking about 40 minutes. If edges brown too quickly, cover with foil strips. Filling should be slightly puffy and golden. Remove from oven and place on wire rack.

3. While pie is baking, prepare topping: In a small bowl, combine nuts, sugar, flour and cinnamon; mix well. Cut in butter with a pastry blender or fork, until mixture forms crumbs the size of peas. Spoon over pie. Bake 15 more minutes or until golden. Remove from oven and cool on a wire rack; serve warm.   10-inch pie

Apple Crisp

This simple and delicious dessert is enhanced with nuts and raisins.

> ¾ cup regular oats
> ¾ cup flour
> 1 cup brown sugar
> ½ teaspoon ground cinnamon
> ½ teaspoon ground nutmeg
> ¼ cup chopped walnuts
> ½ cup butter or margarine
> 4 baking apples (Golden Delicious or Granny Smith) peeled, cored and thinly sliced
> ⅓ cup raisins
> Ice Cream

1. Preheat oven to 350°. In a medium bowl, combine oats, flour, sugar cinnamon, nutmeg and nuts. With a pastry blender or a fork, cut in butter until mixture forms crumbs the size of small peas. Set aside.

2. Arrange apples in a buttered 2-quart baking dish. Sprinkle with raisins. Press the crumb mixture evenly over apples.

3. Bake for 40 minutes or until top is golden and apples are tender. Serve warm with ice cream or cream.   6 servings

Apple Tart

Fresh apples are presented on a flaky crust and highlighted with a golden apricot glaze.

1/2 pound frozen puff pastry, thawed
2 tablespoons sugar
1/4 teaspoon cinnamon
5 crisp baking apples (Golden Delicious, Rome Beauty, Gravenstein)
1/2 lemon
2 tablespoons butter, at room temperature
1/4 cup sliced almonds (optional)
1/2 cup apricot preserves
1/4 cup water
Vanilla ice cream (optional)

1. Roll out puff pastry on a lightly floured board. Place in a 10 or 12-inch pie or springform pan; fold over 1/4-inch to form crust edge. Pierce center bottom of pastry.

2. Preheat oven to 375°. In a small bowl, mix sugar and cinnamon; set mixture aside.

3. Peel and core apples and cut into thin crescents. Squeeze lemon over apples to prevent browning. Arrange on pastry pinwheel fashion, beginning in the center.

4. Sprinkle apples with sugar and cinnamon mixture and dot with butter. Sprinkle with almonds, if desired.

5. Bake tart for 30-35 minutes or until pastry is golden and apples are tender. Remove from oven and cool on a wire rack.

6. Put apricot preserves into blender or food processor; add water and purée. Pour into small saucepan and cook over medium heat until reduced to a glaze consistency.

7. Brush warm glaze over tart. Serve warm with ice cream, if desired.

8 servings

Jane's Chopped Apple Cake

This spicy moist cake keeps well and is delicious with or without frosting. A nice lunchbox or picnic dessert.

> 1/2 cup margarine
> 1 cup sugar
> 1 egg
> 1 teaspoon vanilla
> 1 1/2 cups peeled chopped baking apples (Gravenstein, Golden Delicious)
> 1 teaspoon baking soda
> 1/2 teaspoon salt
> 2 cups all-purpose flour
> 1/2 teaspoon each cinnamon, allspice and nutmeg
> 1/2 cup cold coffee
> 1/2 cup raisins
> 1/2 cup coarsely chopped walnuts
> MOCHA CHOCOLATE FROSTING (see below)
> 1/4 cup finely chopped walnuts (optional)

1. Preheat oven to 350°. In a large mixing bowl, cream together margarine and sugar. Beat in eggs and vanilla; mix in apples.

2. On low speed, add all dry ingredients. Add coffee, raisins and nuts; mix to blend.

3. Pour into a 13x9-inch greased baking pan. Bake for 45 minutes or until toothpick inserted in center comes out clean. (If making cupcakes, bake at 375° for 20 minutes.) Remove from oven and cool on a wire rack.

4. Prepare Mocha Chocolate Frosting and frost, if desired. Additional chopped nuts can be sprinkled on the frosting.   8x8-inch cake

MOCHA CHOCOLATE FROSTING

> 1 (2-ounce) square unsweetened chocolate, melted
> 3 tablespoons hot coffee
> 2 1/2 tablespoons butter or margarine
> 1 1/2 cups confectioners' sugar
> 1/2 teaspoon vanilla

In a medium bowl, beat all ingredients until frosting is smooth and of spreading consistency.

Raspberry Tart

Fresh raspberries are attractively presented on a rich cream filling.

Tart Shell
1/2 cup butter or margarine
1/4 cup sugar
1 teaspoon vanilla
1 large egg yolk
1 1/2 cups all-purpose flour
Cream Filling
2 cups milk
3 egg yolks
2/3 cup sugar
2 tablespoons cornstarch
1/4 teaspoon salt
1 tablespoon butter or margarine
2 tablespoons Kirsch
1 teaspoon vanilla
3 cups fresh red raspberries
Powdered sugar
Whipped cream (optional)

1. To make tart shell: Preheat oven 325°. In a mixing bowl, cream together butter and sugar. Beat in vanilla, egg yolk and slowly add flour; mix well. Press dough into tart or springform pan, covering bottom and making 1-inch sides. Bake for 30 minutes. Remove from oven and cool in pan on wire rack. Remove shell from pan and place on serving platter. Cover tart shell if made ahead.

2. To make cream filling: In a saucepan, over medium heat, scald milk by bringing it to a low simmer; remove from heat and set aside. In a bowl, whisk together the egg yolks, sugar, cornstarch and salt until thick and lemon-colored. Slowly add egg mixture to scalded milk, stirring constantly. Cook over low heat until mixture thickens to consistency of warm pudding; remove from heat. Whisk in butter, Kirsch and vanilla. Cover surface with plastic wrap and let cool. When cooled, pour into tart shell.

3. To assemble tart: Sprinkle berries on cream filling. The tart should be refrigerated for at least 2 hours. Before serving, dust with powdered sugar or serve with whipped cream. 12-inch tart

Wild Blackberry Pie

A true San Juan Islands classic!

Pastry for double-crust, 9-inch pie
3 cups fresh berries, cleaned and hulled
2/3-1 cup sugar
2 tablespoons cornstarch
2 tablespoons butter or margarine
Ice cream (optional)

1. Preheat oven to 400°. Line a pie plate with bottom crust; set aside.

2. In a large bowl, place berries; set aside. In a medium bowl, combine sugar and cornstarch. Pour mixture over berries and toss gently to blend.

3. Pour berry mixture into pie shell; dot with butter. Top with crust and flute edge. Bake for 40 to 50 minutes. If crust browns too quickly, cover with foil strips. Serve with ice cream, if desired.   9-inch pie

Blackberry Crepes Cypress

Don't miss making these mouth-watering crepes when wild blackberries are ripe in July. You can find these delicacies along the road or in logged areas.

Crepes
3 eggs, beaten
2 cups milk
2 tablespoons vegetable oil
2 cups all-purpose flour
Sauce
1 cup wild blackberry jam
1 cup fresh or frozen wild blackberries
1/3 cup butter or margarine
Whipping cream or CREME FRAICHE

1. To prepare crepe batter: In a large mixing bowl, mix all crepe ingredients until batter is the consistency of heavy cream. Set batter aside to rest for 1/2 to 1 hour.

2. To prepare sauce: In a small saucepan, over medium heat, combine jam and berries. If sauce seems too thick, thin with water; keep warm.

3. In a 6 to 8-inch crepe pan, melt 1 teaspoon butter. Pour 2 to 3 tablespoons of batter into pan and tilt to cover pan bottom with a thin layer of batter. Cook crepes until edges are browned; turn and cook other side a few seconds. Remove from pan and place on a warm plate. Repeat steps for more crepes.

4. Spoon about 2 tablespoons of filling into the center of crepe. Roll crepes and place seam-side down. Top with additional sauce and garnish with cream, if desired. 16 crepes

Fresh Strawberry Pie

The charm of this dessert is the combination of a rich, smooth filling and the sweet taste of strawberries.

    1 10-inch baked pastry shell
    2 tablespoons cornstarch
    ¼ cup cold water
    1 cup strawberry preserves
    2 tablespoons lemon juice
    1 (8-ounce) package cream cheese, at room temperature
    1 cup strawberry flavored yogurt
    ¼ cup sugar
    1 teaspoon grated lemon peel
    2 tablespoons lemon juice
    1 quart fresh strawberries, sliced
    1 cup whipping cream

1. In a small saucepan, combine cornstarch and water; add preserves. Bring to a boil and continue stirring. Cook until sauce is thick and clear. Remove from heat and add lemon juice. Set aside to cool.

2. In a medium bowl, combine cream cheese, yogurt, sugar, lemon peel, and lemon juice. Mix thoroughly and spread evenly into baked pastry shell.

3. Top cream cheese mixture with sliced strawberries. When sauce has cooled to room temperature, pour over berries. Cover and chill at least 1 hour. Garnish with whipped cream to serve.   8 servings

Fresh Apricot Torte

Roche Harbor Restaurant serves this irresistible combination of apricots and a creamy custard.

Crust
½ cup butter
7 tablespoons sugar
1½ egg yolks
1½ cups all-purpose flour
4 firm fresh apricots, pitted and cut into thin wedges
Custard
1 egg yolk
3 eggs
¾ cup sugar
1½ cups milk
½ cup whipping cream
2 tablespoons cornstarch

1. In a mixing bowl, beat together butter and sugar until light and fluffy. Add egg yolks and mix well. Lightly beat in flour until mixture is crumbly.

2. Preheat oven to 375°. Press dough into a springform pan, covering bottom and up 1-inch on side of pan. Arrange apricot wedges on crust and set aside.

3. In a medium bowl, combine custard ingredients; beat until well blended. Pour mixture over apricots. Bake for 40 minutes or until knife inserted in the center comes out clean. Remove from oven and cool on wire rack before removing torte from pan.   8-10 servings

Apricot Almond Tarts

These mouth-watering morsels are a delectable dessert to serve company.

Filling
¾ cup diced dried apricots
¾ cup water
½ cup packed brown sugar
½ cup sliced, toasted almonds
2 tablespoons orange liqueur (Grand Marnier, Triple Sec)
Pastry Shells
¼ cup finely ground blanched almonds
¾ cup all-purpose flour
2 tablespoons brown sugar
⅛ teaspoon salt
½ cup butter or margarine
1-2 tablespoons ice water

1. To prepare filling: In a small covered saucepan, simmer apricots in water for 10 minutes. Add brown sugar and continue cooking, uncovered, until thickened, about 10 minutes. Remove apricots from heat, stir in almonds and liqueur; set aside.

2. To prepare pastry shells: Grind almonds in food processor. Add flour, brown sugar and salt; process to blend. Add butter and process until it has the consistency of coarse meal. While machine is running, add water, one teaspoon at a time; continue until a ball begins to form.

3. Preheat oven to 350°. Evenly distribute dough among 20 tart shells. Press balls of dough into shells with fingers, covering bottom and up ½-inch on sides. Spoon about 1 tablespoon of apricot mixture into each tart shell.

4. Bake for 15 minutes or until crust is browned. Remove tart shells from oven and cool for 5 minutes. Carefully remove tarts and place on a wire rack to cool. 20 tarts

Rhubarb Crunch

Celebrate spring with this delicious dessert made with the season's first fruits.

1 1/4 cups flour
1 1/4 cups regular oatmeal
1 cup packed brown sugar
2/3 cup butter or margarine
4 cups diced raw rhubarb (about 1 1/4 pounds)
1 cup sugar
1 cup water
2 tablespoons cornstarch
1 teaspoon vanilla
1/4 cup butter or margarine
Ice Cream

1. Preheat oven to 350°. In a large bowl, combine flour, oatmeal and brown sugar. With a pastry blender or a fork, cut in butter until mixture forms crumbs the size of peas. Press half of the crumb mixture into the bottom of a 2-quart baking dish. Arrange rhubarb on top; set aside.

2. In a medium saucepan, combine sugar, water and cornstarch. Boil until mixture thickens and clears. Remove from heat; add vanilla and butter and stir to melt butter. Pour mixture over rhubarb.

3. Sprinkle remaining crumb mixture over rhubarb. Bake for 50 minutes or until golden. Remove from oven and cool on a wire rack. Serve warm with ice cream.   8 servings

Rhubarb-Orange Custard Pie

Pecans are a crowning touch to this exceptionally tasty pie.

1 9-inch unbaked pie shell
3 eggs, separated
1 1/4 cups sugar
1/4 cup butter or margarine, at room temperature
3 tablespoons frozen orange juice concentrate
1 teaspoon vanilla extract
1/4 cup flour
1/2 teaspoon salt
2 1/2 cups rhubarb, cut into 1-inch pieces
3/4 cup coarsely chopped pecans
Whipped cream (optional)

1. In a large mixing bowl, beat egg whites until stiff, not dry. Add 1/4 cup of the sugar gradually, beating after each addition; set aside.

2. Preheat oven to 375°. In another bowl, beat egg yolks until lemon-colored. Add butter, orange juice and vanilla; beat thoroughly. Beat in remaining 1 cup of sugar, flour and salt.

3. Add rhubarb to yolk mixture; stir to mix. Gently fold in beaten egg whites. Pour into pastry shell and sprinkle with nuts.

4. Bake for 15 minutes on lowest rack. Reduce heat to 325° and bake 45 minutes more. Cover lightly with foil if pie gets too brown. Remove from oven and cool on a wire rack. Top with whipped cream, if desired.

9-inch pie

Chocolate Decadence with Raspberry Sauce

Our version of a popular chocolate-lover's dessert. The tart raspberry sauce compliments the sweetness of the chocolate.

    1 pound bittersweet chocolate
    ¾ cup butter
    1¼ cups sugar
    8 eggs, separated and at room temperature
    2 tablespoons orange liqueur
    1 teaspoon vanilla
    CHOCOLATE GLAZE (recipe follows)
    RASPBERRY SAUCE (recipe follows)

1. In a double boiler, melt chocolate and butter over hot, not boiling, water. Stir in ¾ cup of the sugar and heat until sugar dissolves; set aside.

2. Beat egg yolks in a mixing bowl until frothy. Slowly add ½ cup melted chocolate mixture; beat until well blended. Slowly add the yolk mixture into the double boiler. Stir until mixture thickens, about 4 minutes; remove from heat. Stir liqueur and vanilla into chocolate mixture; set aside.

3. Preheat oven to 350°. In a large mixing bowl, beat whites until almost stiff. Gradually add remaining ½ cup sugar and beat until stiff.

4. Gently fold chocolate mixture into egg whites. Pour into a buttered and sugared 10-inch springform pan.

5. Bake for 30 minutes or until toothpick inserted into center comes out clean. Cool on wire rack before removing cake from pan.

6. Prepare Chocolate Glaze and Raspberry Sauce. Pour glaze over cooled cake and spread evenly.

7. Ladle 2 tablespoons Raspberry Sauce over individual slices and serve.   10-inch cake

CHOCOLATE GLAZE

4 ounces semi-sweet chocolate
2 tablespoons butter
2 tablespoons vegetable oil

1. In a double boiler, over hot water, combine chocolate, butter and oil. Heat until chocolate melts.
2. Remove from heat and allow to cool, about 10 minutes.

RASPBERRY SAUCE

2 cups raspberries
½ cup sugar
½ cup water
1 tablespoon Kirsch (optional)

1. In a medium saucepan, heat to boiling raspberries, sugar and water. Add Kirsch, if desired.
2. Stir to break down raspberries. To remove seeds, strain sauce through a sieve into a bowl. Set aside to cool.   1½ cups

Fresh Fruit with Orange Liqueur

The essence of summer is captured in this colorful combination of mouth-watering fruits.

6 cups assorted fresh fruit (kiwi, blueberries, grapes, strawberries, peaches, pineapple)
½ cup orange liqueur (Grand Marnier, Cointreau or Triple Sec)
CREME FRAICHE (optional – see Index)
¼ cup grated bittersweet chocolate

1. Clean fruit, cut into bite-size pieces and place in a glass bowl. Sprinkle fruit with liqueur and gently toss. Cover and chill until serving time.
2. At the table, ladle fruit and juice into individual glass bowls. Serve with a dollop of Creme Fraiche and a sprinkle of grated chocolate, if desired.

6 servings

Chocolate Orange Trifle

A special dessert served in stemmed glasses at La Petite Restaurant in Anacortes.

2 cups pound cake, cut into bite-size chunks
1 cup fresh squeezed orange juice
2 tablespoons orange liqueur (Grand Marnier)
2 cups heavy cream, slightly whipped and sweetened as desired
8 tablespoons dark Dutch chocolate, shaved

1. Place cake chunks in a medium bowl and toss with orange juice and liqueur; let stand for 2 minutes.
2. Put 1 cup whipped cream in the bottom of each serving glass. Spoon half the pound cake mixture into each glass. Sprinkle each serving with 2 tablespoons of the grated chocolate. Top with remaining cream and garnish with chocolate. Serve immediately.

2 servings

Barkley's White Chocolate Mousse

The ambience and creative cuisine of Barkley's Restaurant of LaConner makes it an ideal choice for a perfect meal. The mellow flavor of this luscious dessert will delight you.

6 ounces white chocolate
3 tablespoons whipping cream
1 teaspoon vanilla
$\frac{1}{4}$ cup brandy
$\frac{1}{8}$ cup sugar
3 egg whites, room temperature
$1\frac{1}{2}$ cups whipping cream
Whipped cream (optional)

1. In a double boiler, melt chocolate over hot, not boiling, water. Remove from heat; stir in 3 tablespoons cream and vanilla. Set aside.

2. In a small saucepan, heat brandy and sugar to boiling. Remove from heat and stir into chocolate mixture.

3. In a large mixing bowl, beat egg whites until stiff but not dry. Gently fold chocolate mixture into egg whites.

4. Whip the $1\frac{1}{2}$ cups cream until stiff, and fold into chocolate mixture. Pour into individual parfait glasses; cover and chill at least 4 hours. Garnish with whipped cream, if desired. 6-8 servings

Chocolate Hazelnut Torte

This irresistible torte is served by one of Guemes Island's finest cooks. The delicate richness will impress the most discriminating palate.

Torte layer
9 eggs, separated and at room temperature
1 1/2 cups granulated sugar
1/3 cup golden rum
1/2 pound shelled hazelnuts, 2 1/2 cups ground (walnuts or a combination can be substituted)
Buttercream filling
1 1/2 cups confectioners' sugar
1 1/2 cups sweet butter, softened
1/4 cup golden rum
3 egg yolks
4 squares unsweetened chocolate, melted and cooled slightly
Frosting
3 squares semi-sweet chocolate
3 tablespoons whipping cream
1 tablespoon rum

1. To prepare torte layers: In a large mixing bowl, beat the 9 egg whites until soft peaks form. Gradually beat in 1 cup of sugar. Continue beating until stiff peaks form; set aside.

2. Preheat oven to 350°. Line bottom of 3 (9-inch) layer cake pans with waxed paper.

3. In a medium bowl, beat egg yolks with remaining 1/2 cup sugar until thick and lemon colored, about 3 minutes; stir in rum. Grind nuts to the consistency of fine meal and add to egg yolk mixture.

4. With a rubber scraper, fold yolk mixture into egg whites. Turn into prepared cake pans. Bake for 30 minutes or until surface springs back when lightly pressed. Let cool in pans on wire racks. Centers of cakes may sink slightly.

5. To prepare filling: In a mixing bowl, combine sugar, butter, rum and egg yolks; beat until well blended. Add melted chocolate and beat again; set filling aside.

6. To prepare frosting: In a double boiler, melt frosting ingredients over hot, not boiling, water. Remove from heat and allow to cool. Frosting should

have the consistency of thick mayonnaise. If frosting is too thin, reheat and add ½ square of semi-sweet chocolate.

7. To assemble torte: Carefully loosen cooled torte layers from pans and peel off waxed paper. Put layers together using about ½ cup filling between each layer. Set aside ½ cup filling for decoration if desired. Spread remaining filling on side of torte. Spread top with frosting. Refrigerate 1 hour or until firm enough to cut.

8. If you want a real show stopper, put reserved filling in pastry bag with a number 30 star tip and pipe rosettes around the top edge of torte. Place whole hazelnuts on top of torte and pipe a border of filling around each. Press chopped hazelnuts against sides of torte. Refrigerate 1 hour or until firm enough to cut.   16 servings

Holly B's Brandy Brownies

A popular stop on Lopez Island is Holly B's Bakery. These rich brownies are just a sampling of her special treats.

2 ounces sweet chocolate	¼ cup instant coffee granules
1 cup butter	1½ cups flour
¾ cup packed brown sugar	½ teaspoon salt
2 eggs	1 teaspoon baking soda
2 tablespoons brandy	1 cup chocolate chips
1 tablespoon vanilla	1 cup coarsely chopped walnuts

1. Preheat oven to 350°. In a double boiler, over hot water melt chocolate. Set aside to cool.

2. In a large mixing bowl, cream together butter and sugar. Add eggs, brandy and vanilla. Mix until smooth, then add reserved chocolate, coffee, flour, salt and soda. Fold chocolate chips and walnuts into flour mixture.

3. Spread batter into a greased 13x9-inch pan. Bake for 15 to 20 minutes or until edges are set and middle jiggles. Do not overbake; brownies will be moist.

20 servings

Chocolate Walnut Pie

This easy-to-make pie served at the New Bay Cafe on Lopez Island will please any chocolate lover.

    1 9-inch unbaked pie shell
    ½ cup butter
    1¼ cups sugar
    ½ cup light corn syrup
    8 ounces semi-sweet chocolate chips
    3 eggs, slightly beaten
    1 teaspoon vanilla
    1½ cups coarsely chopped walnuts
    Whipped cream (optional)

1. Preheat oven to 425°. Bake pie shell for 3-4 minutes; remove from oven and set aside. In a saucepan, combine next 4 ingredients and cook over low heat until chocolate is melted; do not boil. Cool slightly.

2. Reduce oven temperature to 375°. Stir eggs and vanilla into chocolate and mix well. Add walnuts and pour into pie crust. Bake for 40-45 minutes. Let cool on wire rack and serve with whipped cream, if desired.

9-inch pie

Creme Fraiche

This versatile cream can be used with fresh berries, salad dressings, vegetables and soups.

    1 cup heavy cream
    1 cup sour cream

1. In a medium bowl, whisk together heavy cream and sour cream; cover loosely with plastic wrap. Let stand in a moderately warm room overnight to thicken.

2. In the morning, tightly cover and refrigerate for at least 4 hours before using. The fraiche will have thickened. It will keep up to 2 weeks in the refrigerator.

2 cups

Low Calorie Creme Fraiche

Creme fraiche with a slightly tangy flavor.

    1 cup low-fat plain yogurt
    1 cup light cream

Follow directions for Creme Fraiche.   2 cups

Chilled Zabaglione Cream

This is a favorite dessert at La Famiglia Ristorante, one of the most popular restaurants on Orcas Island. This delectable cream can be prepared a day or two in advance.

    6 tablespoons sugar
    1 teaspoon unflavored gelatin
    ½ cup Marsala wine (or dry sherry)
    6 eggs, separated
    1 tablespoon brandy
    1 teaspoon vanilla
    1 cup whipping cream
    ⅛ teaspoon each salt and cream of tartar
    ½ ounce semisweet chocolate, cut in curls or grated

1. In a double boiler, mix together 4 tablespoons sugar and gelatin; stir in wine. In a small bowl, beat egg yolks until foamy; stir into gelatin mixture. Cook over hot, not boiling, water, whisking until thick. Remove from heat; let cool slightly and add brandy and vanilla. Cover and chill about 10 minutes; do not allow to set-up.

2. In a mixing bowl, beat whipping cream until stiff and fold into egg custard. In a clean mixing bowl, beat 3 egg whites until foamy. Reserve remaining 3 egg whites for another use. Add salt and cream of tartar and beat until stiff. Beat in remaining 2 tablespoons sugar.

3. Fold meringue into egg custard. Spoon into parfait glasses. Cover and chill at least 1 hour. Garnish with chocolate curls or fresh berries.

                                                    6-8 servings

Great Rice

Serve this pleasing easy-to-make dessert on a winter evening before a cozy fire.

3 cups milk
¾ cup long grain brown rice
2 tablespoons sugar
1 teaspoon vanilla
½ cup blanched and chopped almonds
1 (16-ounce) can pitted sweet cherries, drained (reserving ½ cup liquid)
1 tablespoon cornstarch
1 tablespoon Kirsch
1 cup heavy cream, whipped

1. In a large saucepan, bring milk to a boil; stir in rice. Reduce heat to low and cook covered, 45 minutes; stir occasionally. Remove from heat, add sugar, vanilla and almonds to rice and milk mixture. Cover and refrigerate 1 hour.

2. Prepare sauce while rice is cooling. In a medium saucepan, combine ½ cup cherry juice with cornstarch, stir until well blended. Stir in drained cherries and cook over medium heat until clear. Remove from heat and stir in Kirsch.

3. Fold whipped cream into rice. Spoon rice into individual serving dishes and top with warm cherry sauce. Serve immediately.

6 servings

Rice Custard

This comforting dessert is perfect for a rainy day.

2 eggs
2 cups milk
⅓ cup sugar
1 teaspoon vanilla
½ teaspoon salt
¾ cup cooked rice
½ cup raisins
Cinnamon
Light cream (optional)

1. Preheat oven to 325°. In a large bowl, beat eggs; add milk, sugar, vanilla and salt. Fold in cooked rice and raisins. Pour into buttered 1-quart baking dish. Sprinkle with cinnamon.

2. Set baking dish in a pan of hot water, 2-inches deep. Bake for 50 to 60 minutes. Custard is ready when knife inserted in the center comes out clean.

3. Let custard stand for 10 minutes. Spoon warm custard into serving bowls. Serve with cream, if desired.

4 servings

Nut Tart

This rich dessert was served at a Guemes Island Book Club Meeting and has been a favorite ever since.

Tart Crust
1 1/2 cups all-purpose flour
1/4 cup sugar
10 tablespoons butter, chilled and cut into pieces
1 large egg yolk
1 teaspoon vanilla extract
1 teaspoon cold water
Nut Filling
3 cups whole or coarsely chopped assorted nuts (pecans, walnuts, filberts or almonds)
3 eggs, beaten
1/2 cup honey
1 teaspoon vanilla
1 tablespoon orange liqueur (Cointreau or Grand Marnier)
1/4 cup butter or margarine, melted
Whipped cream

1. To make tart crust: In a large bowl, combine flour, sugar and butter with a pastry blender or fork until flour mixture is the consistency of coarse meal.

2. Preheat oven to 350°. Add egg yolk and vanilla to flour mixture and stir until dough sticks together. Add water, if necessary, to form a ball. Press dough into a 12-inch tart pan making 1-inch high sides.

3. To make nut filling: Place nuts in shallow pan and bake until lightly toasted, about 10 minutes; let cool.

4. In a bowl, combine remaining ingredients; beat well and stir in toasted nuts. Pour nut mixture into tart shell.

5. Bake on bottom rack for 40 minutes or until top is golden brown. Remove from oven and cool on a wire rack. Cut into serving slices and serve with whipped cream, if desired.

12-inch tart

Raspberry Cordial

Enjoy a taste of summer on a cold winter night with this sumptuous liqueur.

3 quarts raspberries, fresh or frozen
2 cups sugar
1 quart vodka

1. In a gallon jar, pour in raspberries and crush, using a large spoon. Add sugar and vodka and mix together. Loosely cover and store in a cool, dark room.
2. Let stand for 8 weeks. Stir every day for the first week.
3. Strain the cordial through a fine sieve. A nylon sock resting in a colander which has been placed in a large pan works best. Do not squeeze the sock, as it will force out pulp and make your cordial cloudy.
4. You may place cordial into decanters at this time for a lovely gift, or for your own enjoyment.
5. If you have the time and want to be sure you will have no sediment on the bottom of your bottles, you may add this step. After it is strained, return cordial to stand in a cool, dark room for 1-2 months. Syphon the cordial into your decanters, using plastic surgical tubing available at any hardware store. Avoid sediment that has gathered on the bottom.!

4-6 pints

Ya Ya's Baklava

The delicate appearance of this rich Greek dessert is always a crowd pleaser. This recipe of Rob Girdis' grandmother is a favorite at Guemes Island potlucks.

Syrup
1 1/2 cups sugar
1/2 cup honey
1 1/2 cups water
1/4 teaspoon ground cinnamon
2 teaspoons lemon juice
Filling
1 (16-ounce) package shelled walnuts, finely chopped
2 tablespoons ground cinnamon
Pastry
1 pound butter
1 pound phyllo pastry, thawed according to package directions

1. To make syrup: In a medium saucepan, combine sugar, honey, water and cinnamon; simmer 8 minutes. Add lemon juice and cook 2 minutes longer. Syrup should be sticky to the touch. Set aside to cool.

2. To make filling: In a small bowl, combine walnuts and cinnamon until blended; set aside.

3. In a small saucepan, over medium heat, melt butter; keep warm.

4. Fold out stack of phyllo sheets; cover surface with towel or plastic wrap to prevent drying. Remove only one sheet at a time.

5. Brush a 12x18-inch pan with butter. Spread a sheet of phyllo into pan and brush with melted butter. Repeat until there are 6 layers of phyllo. Sprinkle one-third of nut filling on the 6th layer. Add 6 more phyllo leaves, again brushing each with melted butter, sprinkle with one-third nut mixture. Repeat this procedure until all ingredients are used, ending with 6 layers of phyllo for the top. Brush top with butter.

6. Preheat oven to 350°. Before baking, cut dough in pan diagonally into 2-inch strips, then cut diagonally again to make diamond shapes.

7. Bake for 45 minutes. Pastry should be golden brown and flaky. Pastry should be dry, not soft, in the middle.

8. Pour cooled syrup over hot pastry. Pour only enough syrup to fill halfway on pastry. Serve warm or cooled. Stand back and watch it disappear!

20 servings

Index